Manage Anxiety by
Mastering the 10 Tools of the
Praise God Toolbelt

P R A I S E | GOD ™

Tools to

Manage

Anxiety

Pamela Cowgill

The

P.R.A.I.S.E. G.O.D.

Toolbelt

P	R	A	I	S	E		G	O	D	TM
P	R	A	I	S	E		G	O	D	
R	E	T	N	E	N		O	T	O	
A	L	T	S	L	E		A	H		
Y	A	I	P	F	R		L	E	S	
	X	T	I		G		S	R	O	
		U	R	T	I			S	M	
		D	A	A	Z				E	
		E	T	L	E				T	
			I	K					H	
			O						I	
			N						N	
									G	

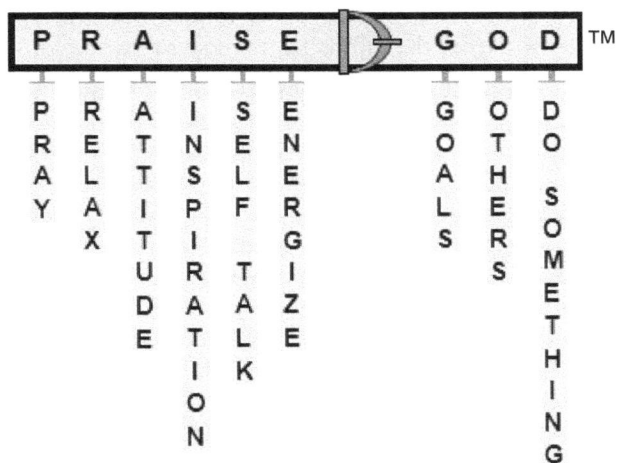

By Pamela Cowgill

Tools to Manage Anxiety[TM]

The Praise God Toolbelt[TM]

Published by

TPGT, LLC
Hilliard, Ohio 43026

Cowgill, Pamela

ISBN 978-0-9787872-9-5 paper

1. Self Help
2. Stress management – Religious aspects – Christianity
3. Worry – Religious aspects – Christianity

2015 First Edition

For information about additional purchases, bulk purchases, or to schedule a workshop, please contact us at our website www.ToolsToManageAnxiety.com or send an email to pamelaj398@gmail.com.

SPECIAL ACKNOWLEDGEMENTS

Ruth Moloney Cowgill

Renee Aitken, Ph.D.

Phillip Hause, Ph.D.

Peg Hays

Disclaimers:

The *Tools to Manage Anxiety* book and the PRAISE GOD TOOLBELT™ were developed as a result of the author's personal experiences.

Statements in this book are not intended to take the place of advice from your mental healthcare and physical healthcare professionals.

This book is neither a cure nor a treatment. The author does not dispense medical advice nor prescribe the use of any technique as a form of treatment and assumes no responsibility for your decisions and actions.

Readers are advised to consult their mental healthcare and physical healthcare professionals to address their specific needs.

This book is not intended to take the place of advice from religious leaders. Readers are advised to consult their Bibles and their religious leaders to address their specific questions or concerns.

Details in some stories may have been changed or omitted to respect the privacy of persons involved.

Scripture quotations are from the King James Version of the Holy Bible. It often uses the male gender as was the custom at the time it was written. I have included gender neutral terms in some places so it refers to all people. The quotations I use are not intended to exclude anyone.

I share what worked successfully for me. The terms anxiety, depression, panic, worry, sadness, distress, fear, hopelessness, stress, etc., are different conditions, but I often use the terms interchangeably. I also experienced a combination. This is not an attempt to define or diagnose those conditions.

I share quotes and references I find thought provoking, enlightening, or interesting. It is not an endorsement of another author's body of work.

Contents

Prologue

Shiny green leaves glistened and fluttered in the breeze outside the window. I blinked and my eyes stung. I must have been staring at the leaves a long time but was only now becoming aware. There was something gritty in my mouth. I reached up and pulled out a piece of tooth. I tried to sit up, but something was holding me down.

"Pam?" I heard my Mother's voice. I looked at her but didn't speak.

"Hello there," she said. I looked around the unfamiliar room – white walls, IVs, a TV perched on a stand above the foot of the bed.

Mom and Dad had been waiting beside my hospital bed praying I would wake up and be all right.

I tried to speak but my mouth was dry, and I was only able to whisper, "What?"

"You had a car accident, but you're going to be just fine."

Why I Created the Toolbelt

In 1984 I was in a car accident that changed my life. Before the accident, I was fearless. I was a singer, and I traveled throughout the Ohio Valley region playing my guitar and entertaining thousands of people. It was a blast. I had so much fun. After the accident and a severe concussion, I lost all my confidence. I became seriously depressed and had panic attacks.

I had no skills to manage this new condition. I did not know how to cope. Through trial and error, I learned what worked for me and what didn't. I called the things that worked "my tools." As time went on, I saw I could arrange the tools in a way that was easy to remember.

I created what I call the Praise God Toolbelt™ so I could remember all the resources and tools available to me to reduce the physical effects of anxiety and stress, to distract myself from obsessive thoughts, and to improve my life by moving forward through difficult situations.

Why I Created this Book

Using the tools made my life better, and I realized other people could also benefit from the toolbelt.

You can use the toolbelt whether you are experiencing difficult times right now, or whether you would like to strengthen yourself with easy-to-use and easy-to-remember tools to use in the future.

Regardless of the cause of your distress, I believe these tools can help you as much as they have helped me. Just like a carpenter uses the right tools to do his or her work, you can use tools in this toolbelt to manage your anxiety so you can do your work and make your life better.

Learning to Manage

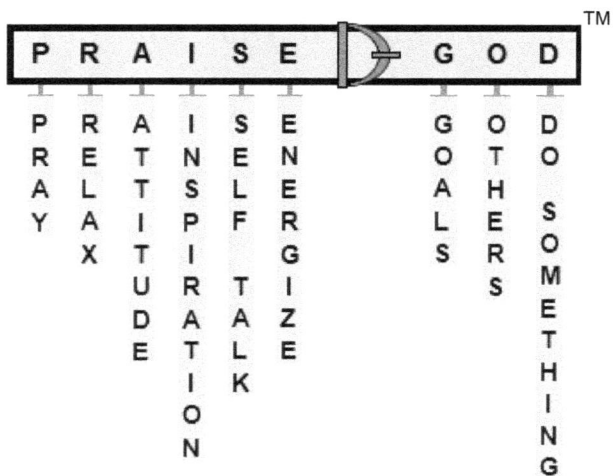

PRAISE — GOD™

P	R	A	I	S	E		G	O	D
P	R	A	I	S	E		G	O	D
R	E	T	N	E	N		O	T	O
A	L	T	S	L	E		A	H	S
Y	A	I	P	F	R		L	E	O
	X	T	I		G		S	R	M
		U	R	T	I			S	E
		D	A	A	Z				T
		E	T	L	E				H
			I	K					I
			O						N
			N						G

Previous life experiences had not prepared me to manage the anxiety, panic attacks, and emotional turmoil I experienced after the car accident. I had to learn how to do that.

Over time, I developed the P.R.A.I.S.E. G.O.D. toolbelt for myself because I needed to be able to quickly remember all the resources available to help me get through problems, calm the anxiety, and quiet my thoughts of hopelessness.

There have been times I was so frustrated and angry with God. But, He never left me. When I would turn to Him, He was always there to let me find another tool, to show me something encouraging, or to bring around the right person who would say what I needed to hear.

"...I will never leave thee, nor forsake thee."
Hebrews 13:5

I've had to learn to trust Him. And, I still use the tools every day because every person alive faces challenges. It's just the way life is. I know I will face more disappointment and heartache but I can face those times with the reassurance God is with me, and I now have the tools I need.

There was a time when I was so miserable. I would work all day, come home and turn on the TV, microwave something for dinner, and fall asleep on the sofa. I wouldn't get a restful eight hours of sleep, and I would go to work tired the next day. I wasn't doing anything to wear myself out, but I was always too tired to do anything else.

Did God want me stressed out and unhappy? No. Was it His plan that I have extreme fear and anxiety and become almost unable to leave the house? No. Did Jesus die on the cross so I could waste my life sleeping on the sofa? *I think not!*

"I am come that they might have life,
and that they might have it more abundantly."
John 10:10

He wants us to participate and have full, abundant lives. We are surrounded by people, pets, and activities to enjoy. Having panic attacks, fear, and extreme anxiety was stopping me from having a full life and robbing me of peace. That was not Jesus' intent.

"Peace I leave with you, my peace I give unto you:
not as the world giveth, give I unto you.
Let not your heart be troubled, neither let it be afraid."
John 14:27

I decided to trust Him. I accepted His gift of peace. I turned to my God and asked for help. When I accepted His help, the tools started to emerge. They just seemed to evolve, one after the other as I needed them. The tools arranged themselves in an easy-to-remember toolbelt. They can be used anytime and anywhere. I use them all the time to manage my daily challenges.

When you find yourself in a stressful situation or you are feeling bad, recognize your feelings as an alert to use the tools to help you cope.

Choose to respond to stress-causing events in a new and different way. Use the tools.

"The significant problems we face cannot be solved
at the same level of thinking we were at
when we created them."
Albert Einstein

Use the tools to change the way you think and change the way you respond, and you can change your life.

You don't need to wait for an appointment, for an event, or for someone else to take action. With all the options and the variety of tools, you can always find at least one tool to help you through any situation – the most important tool is prayer. You can take action right now and at any time without delay to get your life back on track.

In the toolbelt, I join Bible messages with activities, tips, techniques, and resources. Each section is designed with scriptures to reinforce your faith, tools to reduce your anxiety and stress, quotations to expand your thinking, and suggestions to help you take action steps to make your life better.

There is a physical benefit of reducing your stress level:

> *"Stress can cause high blood pressure,*
> *headaches, anxiety, depression,*
> *chest pain and insomnia."* [i]

For me, the tools and the toolbelt became my answer. It has become a powerful resource. It has helped me get closer to God, and it has helped me learn to manage my reaction to problems in my life. It is my pleasure to share the tools with you. If you are struggling with feelings like stress, fear, sadness, distress, worry, hopelessness, or anxiety, regardless of the cause, I believe these tools can help you.

After each chapter, there is a quick summary of tools. Some tools are from the chapter, but there may be additional tools for your consideration.

Summary of Tools from this Chapter

- Keep God's Words in your heart:

  o *"...I will never leave thee, nor forsake thee." Hebrews 13:5*

  o *"I am come that they might have life, and that they might have it more abundantly." John 10:10*

  o *"Peace I leave with you, my peace I give unto you: not as the world giveth, give I unto you. Let not your heart be troubled, neither let it be afraid." John 14:27*

- Let others inspire you.

  o You can choose to change the way you think about and respond to stressful situations: *"The significant problems we face cannot be solved at the same level of thinking we were at when we created them."* Albert Einstein

  o Reduce your stress level for the physical benefits: *"Stress can cause high blood pressure, headaches, anxiety, depression, chest pain and insomnia."* (Union County Health Department)

- These tools are available 24 hours a day, 7 days a week. You can find something in the toolbelt to help you at any time.

- Recognize bad feelings as a signal to use the tools.

- This will prepare you to handle life's challenges: Study your Bible, attend worship services, and learn the tools in the P.R.A.I.S.E. G.O.D. toolbelt.

NOTE: This book is not intended to take the place of your mental healthcare professional nor your physical healthcare professional. Seek their assistance when needed.

Toolbelt Introduction

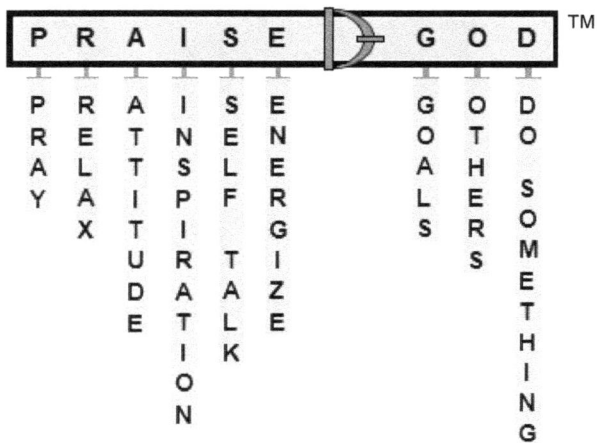

P	R	A	I	S	E		G	O	D |™
P	R	A	I	S	E		G	O	D
R	E	T	N	E	N		O	T	O
A	L	T	S	L	E		A	H	
Y	A	I	P	F	R		L	E	S
	X	T	I		G		S	R	O
		U	R	T	I			S	M
		D	A	A	Z				E
		E	T	L	E				T
			I	K					H
			O						I
			N						N
									G

This toolbelt is full of easy-to-use and easy-to-remember tools for managing anxiety. It is designed to give you the tools to:

- **Reduce** the physical effects of stress and anxiety.

- **Distract** you from stressful thoughts and feelings.

- **Improve** your life by helping you move forward.

This toolbelt centers around the phrase PRAISE GOD, which I use as an acronym – a word or words formed from the first letter of other words. That way, we only have to remember the acronym and the other tools and resources are revealed.

The acronym P.R.A.I.S.E. G.O.D. is the toolbelt that holds all the tools of this program.

Tool #1: PRAISE GOD

This is the starting point. Whatever you are in need of today, reach out to your Heavenly Father.

Praise God to get connected to the Source of help, comfort, power, energy, hope, forgiveness, healing, strength, and love.

Tool #2: Pray

```
P  R  A  I  S  E    ⊃─  G  O  D   TM
P
R
A
Y
```

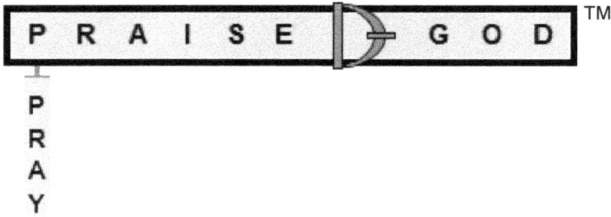

The letter "P" in P.R.A.I.S.E. G.O.D. stands for the tool *Pray*. Prayer can enrich your life, change your perspective, mend your broken heart, and empower you.

Tool #3: Relax

```
P  R  A  I  S  E    ⊃─  G  O  D   TM
P  R
R  E
A  L
Y  A
   X
```

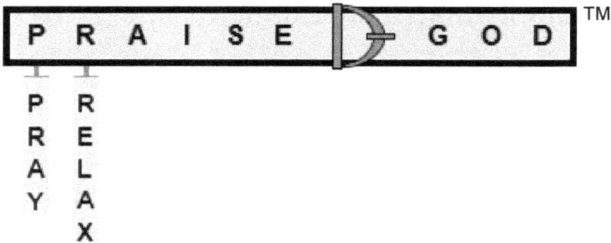

The letter "R" in P.R.A.I.S.E. G.O.D. stands for the tool *Relax*. We will investigate various relaxation techniques.

Tool #4: Attitude

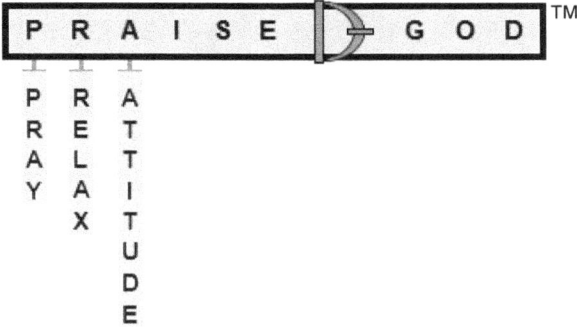

```
┌─────────────────────────────────────────┐
│  P  R  A  I  S  E  [D]─  G  O  D  │ TM
└─────────────────────────────────────────┘
   │  │  │
   P  R  A
   R  E  T
   A  L  T
   Y  A  I
      X  T
         U
         D
         E
```

The letter "A" in P.R.A.I.S.E. G.O.D. is for *Attitude*. There are three tools for this letter.

- The first is the *Attitude of Gratitude*.

- The second is the *Attitude of Faith*.

- The third is the *Attitude of Forgiveness*.

Tool #5: Inspiration

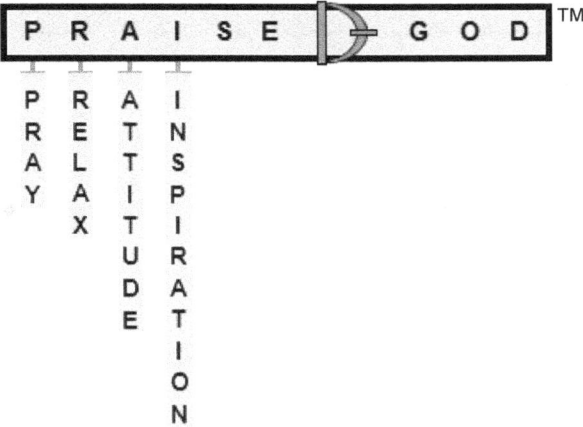

```
┌─────────────────────────────────────────┐
│  P  R  A  I  S  E  [D]─  G  O  D  │ TM
└─────────────────────────────────────────┘
   │  │  │  │
   P  R  A  I
   R  E  T  N
   A  L  T  S
   Y  A  I  P
      X  T  I
         U  R
         D  A
         E  T
            I
            O
            N
```

The letter "I" in P.R.A.I.S.E. G.O.D. stands for *Inspiration*. It refers to inspirational people and inspirational material, such as the Holy Bible, daily devotionals, books, and music.

Tool #6: Self-Talk

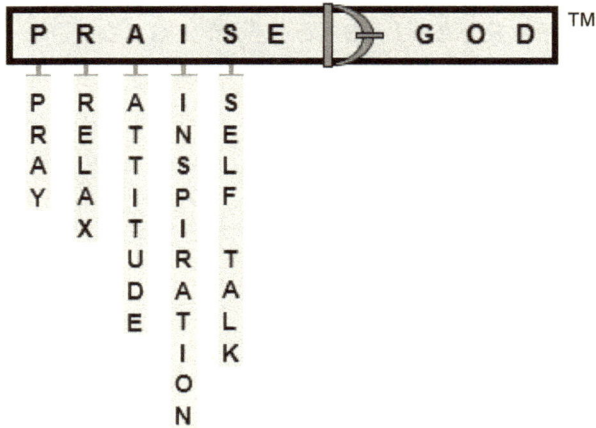

```
P  R  A  I  S  E  [=- G  O  D   TM

P  R  A  I  S
R  E  T  N  E
A  L  T  S  L
Y  A  I  P  F
   X  T  I
      U  R  T
      D  A  A
      E  T  L
         I  K
         O
         N
```

The letter "S" in P.R.A.I.S.E. G.O.D. is for *Self-Talk*. We will look at the words we say to ourselves and how they can be managed.

Tool #7: Energize

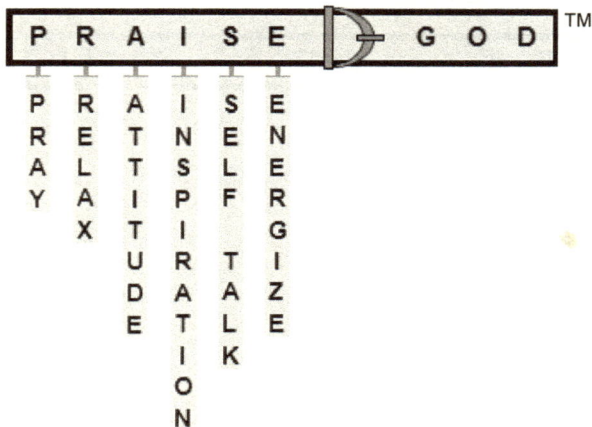

```
P  R  A  I  S  E  [=- G  O  D   TM

P  R  A  I  S  E
R  E  T  N  E  N
A  L  T  S  L  E
Y  A  I  P  F  R
   X  T  I     G
      U  R  T  I
      D  A  A  Z
      E  T  L  E
         I  K
         O
         N
```

"E" represents *Energize*! When our bodies are healthy, we can better handle stress. This part of the toolbelt shares tips and techniques to help you feel better and become energized.

Tool #8: Goals

P	R	A	I	S	E		G	O	D	™

P	R	A	I	S	E		G
R	E	T	N	E	N		O
A	L	T	S	L	E		A
Y	A	I	P	F	R		L
	X	T	I	F	G		S
		U	R	T	I		
		D	A	A	Z		
		E	T	L	E		
			I	K			
			O				
			N				

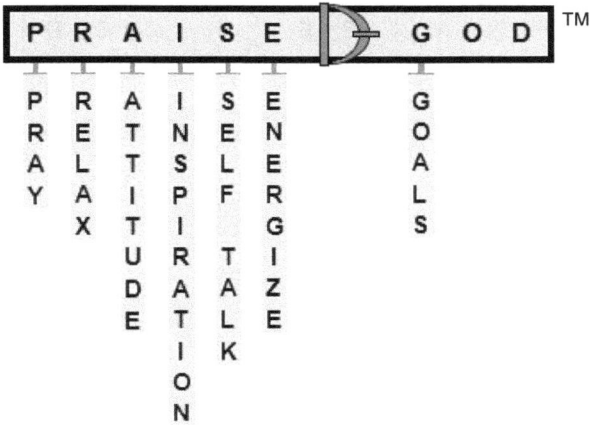

After the belt buckle, the letter "G" in P.R.A.I.S.E. G.O.D. represents *Goals*. This tool is about how setting and accomplishing goals empower us, which helps us manage adversity, anxiety, and stress.

Tool #9: Others

P	R	A	I	S	E		G	O	D	™

P	R	A	I	S	E		G	O
R	E	T	N	E	N		O	T
A	L	T	S	L	E		A	H
Y	A	I	P	F	R		L	E
	X	T	I	F	G		S	R
		U	R	T	I			S
		D	A	A	Z			
		E	T	L	E			
			I	K				
			O					
			N					

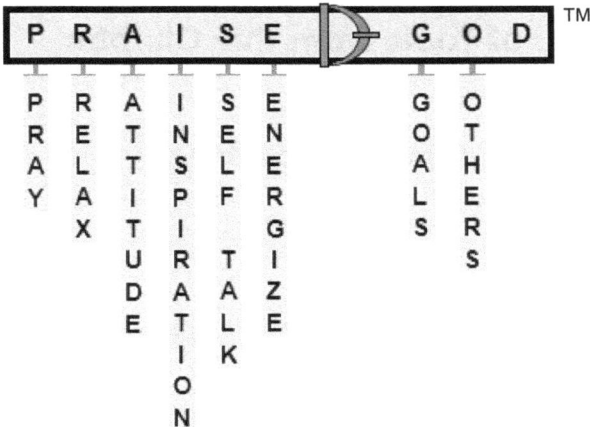

The letter "O" in P.R.A.I.S.E. G.O.D. stands for *Others*. There are two tools here: in *Service to Others* and in *Association with Others*.

Tool #10: Do Something

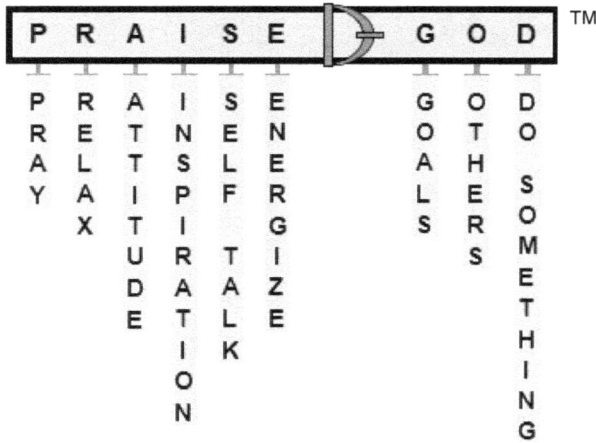

P	R	A	I	S	E		G	O	D	TM

P	R	A	I	S	E		G	O	D
R	E	T	N	E	N		O	T	O
A	L	T	S	L	E		A	H	S
Y	A	I	P	F	R		L	E	O
	X	T	I		G		S	R	M
		U	R	T	I			S	E
		D	A	A	Z				T
		E	T	L	E				H
			I	K					I
			O						N
			N						G

Finally, the letter "D" in P.R.A.I.S.E. G.O.D. is for *Do Something*.

All the tools suggest things you can do or inspirational ways of thinking to help make your life better. The following chapters explore each tool in detail.

Summary of Tools from this Chapter

- Praise God first!

- Then, use the Praise God Toolbelt™.

Tool #1
Praise God

TM

Regardless of the situation, first praise God to get in touch with the Source of help. Whatever you are in need of today, reach out to your Heavenly Father.

"Seek ye first the kingdom of God,
and his righteousness;
and all these things shall be added unto you."
Matthew 6:33

When something happens or you are upset, the first response is "Praise God." Praise God first. Get connected.

"Draw nigh to God,
and he will draw nigh to you."
James 4:8

Praise God to do your part in making a connection with Him from the very beginning. Praise is not an afterthought; make it a constant thought.

My help cometh from the Lord,
which made heaven and earth."
Psalm 121:2

Praise God to get connected to the Source of help, hope, and love.

The phrase "Praise God" helps you remember the acronym P.R.A.I.S.E. G.O.D., which opens the toolbelt.

Summary of Tools from this Chapter

- Keep God's Words in your heart.

  o *"Seek ye first the kingdom of God, and his righteousness; and all these things shall be added unto you."* Matthew *6:33*

  o *"Draw nigh to God, and he will draw nigh to you." James 4:8*

  o *"My help cometh from the Lord, which made heaven and earth." Psalm 121:2*

- Let others inspire you.

  o Continue learning about the tools in the P.R.A.I.S.E. G.O.D toolbelt.

Tool #2
Pray

P R A I S E | G O D ™

P
R
A
Y

In our toolbelt, the letter "P" in P.R.A.I.S.E. G.O.D. holds the tool for *Pray*. Never underestimate the power of prayer.

"The effectual fervent prayer
of a righteous man [person] *availeth much."*
James 5:16

Prayer is very personal. It is a conversation between you and your Maker. I can't tell you how to pray. I would, however, like to share some thoughts about the subject, such as the kinds of prayers, and some scripture to consider.

To start at the top, get down on your knees.
Connect to the Source and pray.

The Kinds of Prayer

The way I see it, the two kinds of prayers are **memorized**, like *The Lord's Prayer*, and **extemporaneous**, where you talk to God in your own words. Different churches seem to favor one or the other. One is not better than the other. Jesus used both. Use both. The only important thing is to pray.

Memorized Prayer. Most Christians are encouraged to memorize *The Lord's Prayer*. Here is what the Holy Bible says in the King James Version:

"Our Father which art in heaven,
Hallowed be thy name.
Thy kingdom come.
Thy will be done in earth, as it is in heaven.
Give us this day our daily bread.
And forgive us our debts, as we forgive our debtors.

And lead us not into temptation;
but deliver us from evil:
for thine is the kingdom, and the power,
and the glory, for ever Amen."
Matthew 6:9-13

This program focuses on a mostly Christian audience (although anyone can use the tools), so you might wonder why I bothered to write out the prayer most of us memorized as children and have said many times. The reason is this: I don't take this prayer for granted, and it is beneficial to take a moment and examine it more closely.

It is beautiful in its simplicity and contains very powerful elements.

1. It praises God and recognizes His holiness.

2. The person praying submits to God's will.

3. It asks Him to fulfill our basic need for food.

4. It asks for forgiveness.

5. It asks for direction and protection.

What could be more perfect? Prayer is the most powerful tool in our toolbelt. Since this is the prayer Jesus taught us, let's look at each of those elements.

- *"Our Father which art in heaven, Hallowed be thy name."*

    This line praises God, offers adoration, and recognizes His holiness. This is also acknowledged in the first part of the toolbelt. The first thing we say is, "Praise God" to get in touch with the Master.

"I will praise thee, O Lord,
with my whole heart"
Psalm 9:1

"Our Father" acknowledges we are part of His family. He is our Father. We are His children.

I miss my Dad. He was a terrific guy and I loved him. Sadly, not everyone knows the love of an earthly father, and I want to recognize the love of our Father in Heaven is different from the love of our Father on earth. The relationship with our Father in Heaven is a spiritual one, and the relationship with our Father on earth is a human one and subject to all the failings of any human relationship.

If the word "father" is difficult for you, use other words. For example, you could always say "Heavenly Father" rather than just "Father" to distinguish between the two. Also, "Abba Father" refers to a more trusting, personal relationship than we could have with another human being.

The point is to acknowledge this is a relationship you deeply respect.

- *"Thy kingdom come. Thy will be done in earth, as it is in heaven."*

The person praying submits to God's will.

In the midst of our struggles, we would do well to humbly accept it as part of God's plan and release the need to control the situation.

> *"Humble yourselves therefore*
> *under the mighty hand of God,*
> *that he may exalt you in due time:"*
> *1 Peter 5:6*

To me, this means I'm to let go of ownership of the problem. I can accept that my will might not be His Will. If I pray and work for a particular outcome and it happens, great. If the outcome I want doesn't happen, I continue to do good where I can[ii] and put the rest in God's hands.

While the outcome I don't want can make me frustrated and angry, some things are beyond my control. I can be at peace if I tried to make things better. And of course, I can't see the situation from God's perspective.

<u>**Thy**</u> will be done.

- *"Give us this day our daily bread."*

The Lord's Prayer asks God to fulfill our basic need for food.

"Or what man is there of you,
whom if his son ask bread, will he give him a stone?"
Matthew 7:9

"Ask, and it shall be given to you;"
Matthew 7:7

In times of disaster, the most immediate need after safety is the need for food and clean water. We cannot live long without it.

In 2005, Hurricane Katrina devastated Louisiana and the Gulf Coast. The suffering was on a massive scale. Food supplies quickly disappeared from stores.

In the 2011 earthquake and tsunami in Japan, hundreds of people stood in long lines to get food and clean water. I watched the reports on TV and heard one young mother saying she was desperate to buy milk for her baby. She was so frightened she couldn't produce breast milk and her baby was in danger of dehydration and possibly death. The need for food and clean water was overwhelming.

There is a chilling story about Stalin forcefully plucking all the feathers from a chicken and then because he would feed the tortured bird, it followed him loyally. The poor bird was starving and endured unbelievable cruelty to get something to eat.

When our bellies are full, we underestimate the need to continually ask our Father to give us our daily bread and to thank God for every meal.

In your prayers, compassionately remember others who struggle daily for basic needs.

- *"And forgive us our debts, as we forgive our debtors."*

In *The Lord's Prayer*, we ask for forgiveness. Stop a minute and think about that. These words are tremendously important.

What is forgiveness? Are you feeling anxiety because you have hurt someone, or someone has hurt you? Forgiveness releases you from pain.

In forgiveness we can:
- Ask God to forgive us.
- Forgive others.
- Forgive ourselves.

Ask God to forgive us. People make mistakes. We hurt others. We break His laws. Our ego takes over sometimes, and we let it. When I acknowledge I have sinned, I take responsibility, and this is very powerful. I hold myself accountable then I humble myself before the Father and sincerely ask His forgiveness. With His help, I have the strength to avoid the same mistakes in the future. He forgives me, and the negative energy disappears. The weight is lifted. His Light fills me with renewed strength.

"...Blessed are they whose iniquities are forgiven, and whose sins are covered." Romans 4:7

Sincerely ask God for forgiveness and you are forgiven.

Forgive others. We are instructed to forgive others, but what does that mean?

> *Then came Peter to him, and said,*
> *Lord, how oft shall my brother sin against me,*
> *and I forgive him? Til seven times?*
> *Jesus saith unto him,*
> *I say not unto thee, Until seven times:*
> *but, Until seventy times seven."*
> *Matthew 18:21-22*

You might be thinking something like, "How can I forgive that person who hurt me? Why would I forgive that scoundrel? Don't you know what she said? Don't you understand what they did?"

Yes, I do understand. In your heart, just forgive them to release the pain you have been carrying. He, she, or they are not in pain. You are in pain. To forgive them is to let go of your pain.

If they have been evil, let God deal with them. Dwelling on how to "get them back" keeps you in a negative state of mind and hurts you, not them. Forgive and forget them, and focus on making your life better.

I don't think it is always necessary for me to have a face-to-face confrontation with someone evil or a person who has hurt me. Sometimes it is. Mainly I believe in forgiving them in my heart, and then I make boundaries so they don't have the chance to hurt me again. What I'm saying about boundaries is I don't purposely put myself in a position where I know I will be abused. We must protect ourselves from cruel behavior.

On those occasions when I must turn the other cheek, so be it.

God forgives us. Likewise, forgive others.

Forgive yourself. I know this is not specifically addressed in *The Lord's Prayer*, but to me it is logical that if I am to forgive someone who has hurt me, sometimes that person is me. Sometimes I need to forgive myself. I replay my mistakes in my head until they become huge. I can really beat up myself. I need to remember when God forgives me, who am I to not forgive myself?

Forgiveness is such a big topic there is more information about it in the section *An Attitude of Forgiveness.*

- *"And lead us not into temptation; but deliver us from evil"*

So, what evil are we talking about? You may have just now gotten an image in your mind of a certain type of evil. There is evil in the world we quickly recognize. It attracts us and tempts us, and we know to avoid it or suffer the consequences. *The Lord's Prayer* asks to be delivered from that kind of evil.

In *The Lord's Prayer* we also ask to be delivered from another kind of evil that is more subtle and can slip into our lives when we are unaware. It is the kind of evil that looks good, and we get involved before realizing the danger.

Here are some examples. There are groups with socially responsible sounding names that have a hidden agenda to try to diminish the importance of our faith. There are "gateway" drugs that are fun and relatively harmless in and of themselves but introduce us to people who actively promote addictive, illegal drugs for their personal profit. There are organizations that ask for donations for a worthy cause but actually use funds for other projects donors would strongly oppose if they knew the truth.

That is the kind of evil we also need to be delivered from – the kind that is not easily identifiable and uses purposefully deceptive tactics.

In *The Lord's Prayer*, we ask specifically and clearly for what we each need and want, including direction and protection. This is so important. There is a lot of bad stuff out there. We are under attack. Don't believe me? The Bible says:

> *"Be sober, be vigilant;*
> *because your adversary the devil,*
> *as a roaring lion, walketh about,*
> *seeking whom he may devour"*
> *1 Peter 5:8*

Those words are as true today as they were 2000 years ago.

Still not convinced? Watch any of the hundreds of movies or shows on TV glorifying lives lived in direct contradiction to living a Christian life. When you watch programs, are *you* being programmed? The purpose of these shows is to ridicule Christian values and glamorize Satan's version of the good life.

Be careful. Stay focused on the Lord.

Here is a poem by Ruth Cowgill capturing this message:

TWO TEAMS

Life is like a football game
Two teams in constant play
Jesus wants His team in heaven
Satan pulls the other way.

Freewill is given to each one
To join a team by choice
With records kept from day to day
Of actions, thoughts, and voice.

And even if we sometimes fill
A place on Satan's team,
We know that Jesus will forgive
Each sin and still redeem.

We cannot change the game of life
No matter how we try
And our freewill choice is taken
The moment that we die.

The goal we choose throughout our life
Of heaven or of hell
Determines for eternity
The place our soul will dwell.

© Ruth Moloney Cowgill

- *"for thine is the kingdom, and the power, and the glory, for ever Amen."*

We worshipfully end *The Lord's Prayer* by giving glory where it is due.

Many people take this magnificent prayer for granted. I used to and then a wedding changed my perspective. At one point in the wedding service the Pastor led *The Lord's Prayer*. I should have closed my eyes and bowed my head as instructed, but I didn't. I was looking around and I noticed one of the bridesmaids was trying to hide the fact she didn't know the prayer. Later at the reception I kept thinking I should talk with her and be friendly. Maybe I could mention the lovely church and nice Pastor, which might have encouraged her to return to the church for a regular service. It bothered me she didn't know *The Lord's Prayer*, which is so basic to my religion. It was in my heart, but I'm ashamed to say I didn't do anything about it.

A few months later I learned she had passed away unexpectedly. I've always felt regret because I could have said something to her. Sometimes I say *The Lord's Prayer* for her because she didn't know it and I could have reached out to her.

"...pray one for another..."
James 5:16

Don't assume others know it. Get some cards printed with *The Lord's Prayer* and leave them wherever you go. What could it hurt? Slip one inside each letter you send (including bills), and make sure you don't live with the guilt that you could have shared this powerful prayer with someone.

The design of my business card has changed several times but here is an idea of what it looks like with *The Lord's Prayer* on the back:

The Praise God Toolbelt

PRAISE → GOD

PRAY | RELAX | ATTITUDE | INSPIRATION | SELF TALK | ENERGIZE | GOALS | OTHERS | DO SOMETHING

pamelaj398@gmail.com

Our Father which art in heaven, Hallowed be thy name.
Thy kingdom come. Thy will be done, as in heaven, so in
earth. Give us day by day our daily bread. And forgive us our
sins; for we also forgive every one that is indebted to us.
And lead us not into temptation; but deliver us from evil.
For thine is the Kingdom,
and the Power, and the Glory forever.

I use memorized prayers when my mind gets stuck thinking about something upsetting. I might be afraid and not thinking rationally, or I might start obsessing. You can't think of two different things at the same time, so I force myself to start praying. It's usually *The Lord's Prayer*, and it breaks the negative thought pattern. It helps me make a connection with God when I'm having trouble.

Pray with your heart. Saying the same prayer or scripture repeatedly isn't "vain repetition" (Matthew 6:7) as long as you pray with sincerity. Pray it; don't just say it.

"This people honoureth me with their lips,
but their heart is far from me."
Mark 7:6

Extemporaneous Prayer. It's also great to hear someone deliver a heartfelt extemporaneous prayer touching the same important elements as *The Lord's Prayer*: Praise Him, tell Him what you need, ask for forgiveness, and ask for protection. Don't forget to thank Him. That's the complete package.

Extemporaneous prayers do not need to be long. A prayer can be one word.

Many years ago I was driving on a narrow road along the Scioto River. I wasn't paying attention and the car tires slipped off the right side of the road onto gravel. It startled me, and I jerked the wheel to the left. The car did a complete 360° spin during which I screamed "JESUS!"

Amazingly, the car came to an abrupt stop. It was as if He put His hand on my car and stopped it. I was shaking. I started to get out of the car to gather my composure but when I opened the door, I was looking straight down a cliff into the icy Scioto River.

I know God stopped my car that day. If my car had skidded a few more inches, it could have been a disaster for me.

When I screamed "JESUS," it was an extemporaneous prayer from the bottom of my heart and soul, and it contained tremendous passion. He filled in the blanks and answered my prayer immediately.

"And it shall come to pass,
that before they call, I will answer;
and while they are yet speaking, I will hear."
Isaiah 65:24

It is wise to have an extemporaneous prayer on the tip of your tongue at all times. Even a one-word prayer will do.

Why Should We Pray?

God already knows what you need, but you need to take action. It is the reaching out to Him that is so important.

The Holy Bible says to pray.

"Be careful for nothing;
but in every thing by prayer and supplication
with thanksgiving
let your requests be made known unto God."
Philippians 4:6

To ask with supplication is to ask humbly.

It is your opportunity to get connected to Him and to keep the lines of communication open.

"Then shall ye call upon me,
and ye shall go and pray unto me,
and I will hearken unto you."
Jeremiah 29:12

Jesus is our example, and he prayed.

"And in the morning,
rising up a great while before day,
he went out, and departed into a solitary place,
and there prayed."
Mark 1:35

How Should We Pray?

Pray with feeling, enthusiasm, energy, and PASSION! Jesus is our example. How did he pray on the Mount of Olives? He prayed with passion.

*"And being in an agony he prayed more earnestly;
And his sweat was as it were great drops of blood
falling down to the ground."*
Luke 22:44

Pray with passion, conviction, and unshakable faith God is listening.

Pray in the secret of your heart with all your heart.

*"But thou, when thou prayest, enter into thy closet,
and when thou hast shut thy door,
pray to thy Father which is in secret;
and thy Father which seeth in secret shall reward thee openly."*
Matthew 6:6

I have spent many hours agonizing, worrying, suffering, and crying about different problems but forgetting to take them to God. My problems would have been solved sooner and my distress relieved had I turned toward the Source of help.

Pray with passion, conviction, and unshakable faith God is listening. Dig deeper into the Word and your feelings. Honor Him with your heart.

When Should We Pray?

Pray always.

*"Evening, and morning, and at noon, will I pray,
and cry aloud: and he shall hear my voice."*
Psalm 55:17

Pray always.

"Watch ye therefore, and pray always..."
Luke 21:36

Pray always.

"Pray without ceasing."
1 Thessalonians 5:17

That last one says it all. Fill your day with prayer and see how it changes your life. Pray without ceasing.

Does God Answer Prayer?

Yes! I know God answered my one-word prayer the day my car spun out of control beside the Scioto River. I know He has answered my prayers to get me through health challenges, financial difficulties, and other life struggles. I asked, and I have received answers to my prayers. Praise God!

"...ask, and ye shall receive,
that your joy may be full."
John 16:23-24

You can pray to Him right now and anytime you need His comfort and guidance. Just ask.

"Ask, and it shall be given you; seek, and ye shall find;
knock and it shall be opened unto you"
Matthew 7:7

Read His promises in the Holy Bible and then look for more books about answered prayer. Right now I am reading *Chicken Soup for the Soul Answered Prayers, 101 Stories of Hope, Miracles, Faith, Divine Intervention, and the Power of Prayer*[iii] by Jack Canfield, Mark Victor Hansen, and LeAnn Thieman. It's delightful.

If you are not familiar with *Guideposts Magazine*[iv], search for it on the Internet. You can spend many hours reading stories about faith, answered prayer, angels, inspiration, and miracles that will touch your heart and strengthen your faith.

Does God answer prayer? Yes and He is only a prayer away.

I came across an interesting book by Masaru Emoto[v] showing the results of his study of the effect of prayer and positive thoughts on ice crystals. He found dirty, polluted water makes ugly, distorted ice crystals. After praying over the same water and sending it positive thoughts and feelings, the water made beautiful crystals. While I don't know how scientific the study was, I believe prayer and positive thoughts do have an affect on things as well as people. I believe prayer can cause change.

If prayer can change water as in Mr. Emoto's study, could it be possible to think prayer causes a change in things containing mostly water – like food? We pray over our food and we focus on giving thanks; but, perhaps there is an additional aspect that the prayers we say somehow change the food so it provides more of what our bodies need. It makes me wonder.

Summary of Prayer Tools from this Chapter

- Keep God's Words in your heart.

  o *"The effectual fervent prayer of a righteous man availeth much." James 5:16*

  o *"Our Father which art in heaven, Hallowed be thy name. Thy kingdom come. Thy will be done in earth, as it is in heaven. Give us this day our daily bread. And forgive us our debts, as we forgive our debtors. And lead us not into temptation; but deliver us from evil: for thine is the kingdom, and the power, and the glory, for ever Amen." Matthew 6:9-13*

  o *"I will praise thee, O Lord, with my whole heart" Psalm 9:1* o *"Humble yourselves therefore under the mighty hand of God, that he may exalt you in due time" 1 Peter 5:6*

o *"Or what man is there of you, whom if his son ask bread, will he give him a stone?" Matthew 7:9*

o *"Ask, and it shall be given to you" Matthew 7:7*

o *"...Blessed are they whose iniquities are forgiven, and whose sins are covered." Romans 4:7*

o *"Then came Peter to him, and said, Lord, how oft shall my brother sin against me, and I forgive him? Til seven times? Jesus saith unto him, I say not unto thee, Until seven times: but, Until seventy times seven." Matthew 18:21-22*

o *"Be sober, be vigilant; because your adversary the devil, as a roaring lion, walketh about, seeking whom he may devour" 1 Peter 5:8*

o *"...pray one for another..." James 5:16*

o *"And it shall come to pass, that before they call, I will answer; and while they are yet speaking, I will hear." Isaiah 65:24*

o *"Be careful for nothing; but in every thing by prayer and supplication with thanksgiving let your requests be made known unto God." Philippians 4:6*

o *"Then shall ye call upon me, and ye shall go and pray unto me, and I will hearken unto you." Jeremiah 29:12*

o *"And in the morning, rising up a great while before day, he went out, and departed into a solitary place, and there prayed." Mark 1:35*

o *"And being in an agony he prayed more earnestly; And his sweat was as it were great drops of blood falling down to the ground." Luke 22:44*

- o *"But thou, when thou prayest, enter into thy closet, and when thou hast shut thy door, pray to thy Father which is in secret; and thy Father which seeth in secret shall reward thee openly."* Matthew 6:6

- o *"But when ye pray, use not vain repetitions, as the heathen do: for they think that they shall be heard for their much speaking."* Matthew 6:7

- o *"This people honoureth me with their lips, but their heart is far from me."* Mark 7:6

- o *"Evening, and morning, and at noon, will I pray, and cry aloud: and he shall hear my voice."* Psalm 55:17

- o *"And he spake a parable unto them to this end, that men ought always to pray, and not to faint"* Luke 18:1

- o *"Watch ye therefore, and pray always..."* Luke 21:36

- o *"Pray without ceasing."* 1 Thessalonians 5:17

- o *"...ask, and ye shall receive, that your joy may be full."* John 16:23-24

- o *"Ask, and it shall be given you; seek, and ye shall find; knock and it shall be opened unto you"* Matthew 7:7

- o *"...I will never leave thee, nor forsake thee."* Hebrews 13:5

- Let others inspire you.

  - o To start at the top, get down on your knees. Connect to the Source and pray.

  - o *"The most effective prayers are usually the simple prayers."* Joyce Meyer

- The "P" in the acronym P.R.A.I.S.E. G.O.D. reminds us to pray.

- Never underestimate the power of prayer.

- Pray in your own way. This is your personal conversation with God.

- Pray from your heart. Pray with feeling, enthusiasm, energy, and passion.

- Use memorized prayers to help when you are stuck.

- Memorize *The Lord's Prayer*.

- Have an extemporaneous prayer on the tip of your tongue at all times.

- Say a prayer of thanks at each meal.

- In your prayers, compassionately remember others who struggle daily for basic needs, like clean water and food.

- Pray to glorify God.

- Pray with passion, conviction, and unshakable faith.

- Pray for forgiveness.

- Forgive yourself.

- Forgive others quickly.

- Forgive others to release your pain.

- Pray for others.

- Pray for protection. Realize you are under attack and be vigilant. Fortify your faith with prayer.

- Use prayer as an opportunity to really connect with God. Talk to Him and pray for His guidance.

- Pray always.

- Accept sometimes our will is not His Will and leave difficult situations in His hands.

- Fill your day with prayer and see how it changes your life.

- Share *The Lord's Prayer* with friends, family, and strangers. Get a business card printed with *The Lord's Prayer* and leave them everywhere. God will put them in the hands of the people who need them. It is not necessary to add your contact information on the card. *The Lord's Prayer* already shows God's contact information.

Tool #3

Relax

PRAISE – GOD ™

P R
R E
A L
Y A
    X

The letter "R" in our P.R.A.I.S.E. G.O.D. acronym stands for the tool *Relax*.

Anxiety is not just a thought. There is also a physical reaction. Often when I'm stressed and anxious, my body reacts. My shoulders and neck will be tight and achy, my breathing will be shallow, and my heart will be racing. The emotion of stress can cause the physical body to feel stress and likewise a relaxed body helps relax the mind. Some people question the mind/body connection but think about it: Do you blush when embarrassed? Do you cry when sad? These are examples of your body reacting to emotion and thoughts running through your mind.

In the previous sections, you praised God to get in touch with the Source of help. You prayed and put your situation in God's hands. You have done what is needed to resolve anything and everything. It's in God's hands.

Now it is time to relax your body. Since you still have your motor running in high gear and stress-related chemicals[vi] are rushing through your body, you need to slow that down.

> *"And to you who are troubled rest with us..."*
> *2 Thessalonians 1:7*

In this section, we will look at relaxation tools and tips to:
1. Relax your muscles and your mind
2. Remove stressors
3. Redirect your attention

Relax Your Muscles and Your Mind

Coax your body into relaxing with:
- Controlled breathing
- Progressive (guided) relaxation
- Massage

Controlled Breathing. When I'm anxious or stressed, my breathing is quick and shallow, and my heart is racing. Controlled breathing helps me.

I consciously slow my breathing. I breathe in slowly through my nose then I breathe out slowly through my mouth focusing on the warm air as it leaves my body. I do this a couple times. I often feel my racing heart slow down and becoming calm. It also gives me a quick mental break because my focus is redirected.

I find it helps to drop my shoulders and roll my head from side to side to release the tension.

Progressive (Guided) Relaxation. I started using guided relaxation after attending a seminar by Marshall Sylver[vii] in about 2002. Mr. Sylver has a subconscious reprogramming recording for weight loss that starts with excellent guided relaxation.

I listened to the recording at bedtime for many months to relax, and the results were amazing. I would turn on the tape, and when I heard his soothing voice, my body would completely relax, and I'd fall asleep. Hours later I'd awaken totally refreshed.

I learned I could use guided relaxation to teach my body to relax one area at a time, and you can learn to do this too. I designed a procedure that works for me, and it is outlined below. The more I went through the procedure, the easier it became and the more deeply I was able to relax. The ability to relax my body became an automatic response.

This is the procedure I use:

1. I go to a quiet place and get in a comfortable position.

2. I close my eyes and mentally focus on *one muscle group or area at a time*. I do this slowly. Always start from the toes and work up **or** start from the head and work down. Once you decide the direction, don't change because consistency is important.

3. I think to myself, "My muscles are relaxing. God's warmth, love, and peace flow into my body."

4. I picture His love gently drifting down to me from heaven. God's healing power lingers at each area that needs His help. Muscles loosen and become calm.

5. I whisper to myself, "I fall asleep easily."

6. I relax in the knowledge I am in His care. There is nothing He can't handle. I am safe and at peace.

Pay attention to the wording:

Don't say "I'm going to fall asleep" because "going to" is in the future, and the future is always in the future. Instead say, "I fall asleep easily."

Use positive messages. Don't say, "I am not stressed." Say, "I am completely relaxed."

When my mind wanders, I simply refocus and continue the guided relaxation.

This procedure can be useful in helping you fall asleep at night but once learned, it can be modified to help you relax anytime you feel anxiety. For example, I always use it in the dentist's office, which is a stressful place for me.

If you would like to try this, read through the procedure a couple times then lie down and go through it in your mind. Think "peace." Think "slow down." The more you let yourself focus on the procedure and feel each muscle or muscle group relax, the more you will benefit from this exercise. Do this *slowly* and *thoughtfully*. I found when I did this night after night, relaxing my muscles became easier.

> *"Come unto me,*
> *all ye that labour and are heavy laden,*
> *and I will give you rest."*
> *Matthew 11:28*

When I have trouble sleeping due to physical pain, I visit my Chiropractor.

Massage. A massage can relax your muscles and your mind. It relaxes muscles by manipulation, and it relaxes your mind because it keeps you in the present moment, and you cannot think about anything else.

Massage can improve circulation and relieve muscle pain and stiffness. Many people find it refreshing.

There are several different techniques so you may have to do some research and ask some questions to find what you need. I am familiar with these techniques:

- A simple massage involves the therapist using oil or lotion and massaging the body with gentle smooth or circular strokes. I found having a massage very helpful when I needed work on sore, injured muscles. This worked out a lot of muscle pain but, this kind of massage doesn't relax me because I'm somewhat of a touch-me-not. However, other people have told me they enjoy this kind of massage.

- Some therapists offer back massages. Where I worked at AT&T, there was an exercise room, and employees could schedule a 15 minute back massage in the middle of the work day. It was great. The therapist used a specially designed chair where you could sit and lean forward, and he would massage your neck, back, and shoulders. Since this type of massage is done through your clothing, it can be done in public areas. To me, this was very relaxing.

- My Dad did a type of acupressure massage. It is done using finger pressure on acupuncture points. This is done without needles. Finger pressure on the right spot can relieve pain or reduce anxiety. I don't know how it works, but it worked on me. I remember being very anxious about something and Dad showed me how to apply pressure and rub a spot on the web between my thumb and first finger. Oddly enough, when I was anxious, there was a place there that would be sore. As I massaged the spot, it reduced my anxiety.

- Foot massage is called reflexology. Don't worry about being ticklish, it isn't like that. The reflexologist massages each foot. If there are sore spots, he or she works on that area to relieve the pain. I've had a couple of these. The most recent was at a health fair.

  I also have a reflexology ball under my desk at home and use it all the time. It's a ball about 5 inches across, and it's covered with bumps. I roll the ball under my feet while working. When I find a sore spot, I massage it a little longer. It helps.

If you think you would like to try a massage but have uncertainties, ask your doctor if he or she can recommend a licensed massage therapist.

Remove Stressors

Get rid of or manage some upsetting stressors such as:
- Endless chores
- Stressful media
- Offensive or difficult people
- Intimidating people
- Wrong perspective

Endless Chores. Remove the stress of running seven days a week and give yourself a day of rest. We live in a society where we have forgotten:

"Six days shall work be done:
but the seventh day is the Sabbath of rest,
an holy convocation; ye shall do no work therein;
it is the Sabbath of the Lord in all your dwellings."
Leviticus 23:3

"An holy convocation" means a formal assembly of people, which I understand to mean a church service.

I remember when stores and restaurants were not open on Sunday. That day was set aside for church, family, and rest.

Today many of us run to work Monday through Friday, and then run all weekend to fit in laundry, household chores, grocery shopping, family needs, sports activities, and other commitments. It seems like all we do is run just to try to break even. The list of what we need to do plays non-stop in our minds and sometimes overlooked items pop in our heads in the middle of the night, robbing us of sleep.

I'm guilty of this. My job is tough, and I work long hours. Monday through Friday I go to work then come home. That's it. Sometimes I can fit in something else, but not often. That leaves Saturday and Sunday to do the chores and to have a life. I often feel like I'll never catch up.

There are so many activities filling up every day, often the most important things, like rest and spiritual needs, are neglected. It takes some planning and letting go, but it is critical to reschedule chores and set aside a true day of rest for you and your family.

Here are some hints that might help with organizing, prioritizing, and scheduling tasks.

In the evening, I make a short list of the important things I need to do the following day. Then I number the list in order of importance. The next day, I tackle the most important item on the list first. Then, I work my way through the list. Items that have not been completed can move to the list for the following day, can be assigned to someone else, or can be eliminated. You can reduce your stress by knowing the most important things are getting done, and you are not being distracted by less important tasks.

Each night there will be new items for your list. Again, prioritize the items and the next day start with the most important task first.

This will stop those forgotten items from popping in your head when you are trying to sleep. They are all captured on your list.

Here is an example of what I mean:

Friday
__1__ Check on Mrs. Neighbors.
__2__ Pick up dry cleaning.
__3__ Do laundry.
__4__ Get the oil changed.

Perhaps Mrs. Neighbors is ill and needs my help. If it is all I get done on Friday, at least I have done the most important thing. Maybe I also have time to pick up the dry cleaning and start the laundry. The rest of the laundry and the oil change move to the list for the next day.

On Friday night, I make a list for Saturday.

Saturday
__1__ Plan meals for Sunday.
__2__ Finish laundry.
__3__ Sew a button on a jacket.
__4__ Get the oil changed.

The #1 thing on this list is to plan meals on Saturday to enjoy on Sunday so I can spend less time working in the kitchen on Sunday.

Finishing the laundry is now the second task.

An unexpected task is now on the list. It seems someone has lost a button on a jacket. You have some options. You can sew on a new button, or you could teach that person how to sew on a button. Consider reducing your workload and empowering others by teaching them useful life skills. It is a disservice to not teach others to do things for themselves.

Teach life skills to your children from a young age so they can be self-reliant, capable, and confident. Life skills include basic cooking, cleaning, home maintenance, car maintenance, and good work habits.

Determine if you are overworked and experiencing stress because someone is taking advantage of you, and you are allowing it. That isn't love; it's called co-dependency. Everyone needs to participate in his or her fair share of household and life responsibilities.

It is important to identify what "rest" means to your family and how that can be accomplished. You may have a spouse or children who define their day of rest as one that has you waiting on them hand and foot. There may need to be a family discussion to determine how everyone can have a day of rest.

On the list, the oil change is item #4. It is not critical at this point so it can wait until Monday. If not taken care of soon, it will become critical then it will be higher on the list.

The top priorities on your list for Sunday are worship, rest, and spending time with the people you love.

It is not unusual for me to start one task then change to another without finishing the first. A list helps me focus and complete an important task, cross it off the list, and then move on. Not only do I get more done, but there is also a feeling of accomplishment when I cross off each task.

Notice the list is short and manageable. A long list makes me feel overwhelmed. A short, prioritized list reduces my stress level. The objective is to fit in all the important tasks and keep a day of rest reserved so I can recharge physically and spiritually.

Stressful Media. Another way to remove stressors in your life is to *manage* entertainment media, such as TV, movies, computers, radio, computer games, or music.

While there are many types of entertainment media, the problems are pretty much the same. Each one can be a nice way to relax; however, any one of them can be the source of unnecessary stress.

You already know the good part of entertainment media. It's fun and it makes you feel good. It can be a good distraction and very relaxing. I'm not saying to stop doing what you enjoy. Just learn to recognize when it raises your anxiety level and learn to manage the activity.

Keep in mind:

"Moderation in all things."
Andria Terence, Roman Comic Dramatist,
(185 BC – 159 BC)

- Entertainment media can steal your time.

    TV takes up a lot of our time, and too much can be a problem. It can be enlightening to keep a log of how much time you spend watching TV. When I am depressed, I find I watch a lot of TV. The more TV I watch, the more depressed I become. It's an emotional downward spiral. It seems most programs are either news (which is always bad); sports (which I believe gets too much emphasis); reality shows (which have nothing to do with reality as I know it); murder, detective, or mystery shows (which usually start with something gruesome that nightmares are made of); or shows that glamorize living a lifestyle that does not reflect my values.

    Of course, there are some good shows. I like to relax in front of the TV, just like you. It's compelling. But, I find if I don't stay aware of the time, I can sit there and watch all evening when there are other things needing my attention. When I reduce my time watching TV, my house gets cleaned, I accomplish more goals, my life is better organized, and THAT reduces my stress level.

    The best technique for me is to set aside certain days when the TV will be off all day.

    Because TV was causing me a lot of unnecessary anxiety at one point, I put the TV in the garage for a year as an exercise in self-discipline. It was an interesting year and I really didn't miss anything. If there was important news, people would tell me.

Like TV, computers and gaming systems can eat up time. Playing games can be a problem when it's hard to stop. It can turn into a bad habit or even an addiction. Enjoy your computer and games but be aware of the time spent in unproductive activities.

- Entertainment media can stop you from accomplishing your goals.

What do you want for your life? Entertainment media takes time that could be used towards accomplishing the real desires of your heart.

- Entertainment media can make you physically unhealthy.

You may have heard the expression, "couch potato." That's when someone spends a lot of time sitting and doesn't get enough physical activity. They start packing on extra weight. After a day of limited physical activity like sitting at a desk, sitting in the car, and an evening of sitting in front of the TV or computer, the body gets sluggish and out of shape. We feel better and sleep better when we have more physical activity.

- Entertainment media can rob you of sleep.

News, action shows, timed computer games, tactical computer battle games, and intense movies affect your body. An earlier section about guided relaxation explained how what goes on in your mind affects your body. You have physical responses from thought.

On TV, your mind sees horrible events. That triggers a fight, flight, or freeze response in your body to some degree. You don't sit there watching completely unaffected.

Whether it is real like the news or imitation like a movie, your mind takes it all in just the same. I find myself crying at sad stories and laughing at funny shows. I might even notice my breathing becoming quick and shallow while watching the action of a battle. Logic tells me it is not real, but my body still reacts.

Watching exciting or stressful shows before bedtime can rob you of sleep because the stress chemicals are still racing through your body.

- Entertainment media can wreck your body's natural clock.

Light affects melatonin production, which is a chemical naturally produced by the body to make us feel sleepy.[viii] Light reduces the amount of melatonin produced by the body.

When you stare into a bright screen just before going to bed, it fools your body into reacting like it is daytime.

I don't have a TV or computer in my bedroom because of the bright screen. I keep my room dark at night, which helps my body fall asleep naturally.

If you have trouble falling asleep, consider making your bedroom dark and removing anything with a screen. View TV or computer screens earlier in the day to see if that solves the problem.

- Entertainment media can become a replacement for having social contacts.

We can get in the habit of watching TV and developing artificial relationships with the characters we see. Many people schedule their lives around their favorite programs and will choose TV over socializing with real people. If we had no TV and we wanted human interaction, we might make more of an effort to visit with others and build relationships. A wide, diverse circle of friends and acquaintances can enrich our lives and make us feel more in touch with our neighbors, church family, coworkers, and community, which can help us feel more secure and therefore, less stressed. In times of trouble, they are our comfort and support, not TV characters.

Also, the friendship with real people can't be canceled by the network at the end of the season.

On the other hand, we can use the computer for social networking. I'm amazed at the number of people who are finding websites to reconnect with people they haven't heard from in years, which I think is wonderful. I am always delighted to find people I haven't seen since high school. A few years have passed, but I'm still 16 at heart and happy to find classmates once more.

- Entertainment media can make you feel bad about yourself.

  Are you being programmed by entertainment media to feel bad? There are laws regulating the hidden subliminal messages media companies send you because they are too effective, but there are other messages hidden in plain sight about all the things you *need* to buy. This adds a lot of stress if you keep getting the message you are not good enough because you don't have this or that item. It increases anxiety if don't have extra money for their products. Don't allow marketing techniques to make you feel bad about yourself.

  Are you being influenced and programmed? Apparently advertisers believe so. According to Forbes, in 2014 a 30-second Super Bowl commercial costs about $4 million.[ix] They would not spend that kind of money on advertising if it wasn't effective.

Enjoy the funny Super Bowl commercials but be aware of the powerful messages directed at you through entertainment media for their profit (not necessarily for your good) and make your own decisions about what you want to be, do, or have.

- Some entertainment media, like music, can be relaxing, or it can increase your stress level.

Manage your music. Become aware of how it affects your body and use it for your benefit. If you need to blow off steam, listen to rock. If you need to relax, listen to something soothing. Intentionally play music to set the mood you want rather than simply reacting to whatever is played.

I like classic rock, but sometimes I find listening to rock music increases my stress level when I don't need that. One of the most powerful mood changers for me is to change the channel on the radio from stress-inducing news or rock to smooth jazz or Southern Gospel. One minute I'm gripping the steering wheel and being anxious and then the next minute I'm gliding down the highway completely happy. I often miss cell phone calls because I'm lost in the music. When a song comes on I know, I sing at the top of my lungs. Why not? It's fun!

"Sing aloud unto God our strength:
make a joyful noise unto the God of Jacob."
Psalms 81:1

Make a "joyful" noise. Notice it doesn't say anything about singing on key or knowing all the words.

I heard a loveable old pastor jokingly say, "If God gave you a nice voice, sing loud to thank Him. If He gave you a bad voice, sing loud and pay him back. Either way, sing!"

"The Lord is my strength and song..."
Exodus 15:2

<u>Offensive or Difficult People</u>. I know this can be a challenge, but learning to manage offensive or difficult people in your life can pay off by reducing your stress level.

I have encountered difficult people every place, at every job, in every group, in every neighborhood, in every family, and so forth. Before you say **I** am the common denominator in this equation so I must be the difficult one, I believe difficult people are in everyone's life to some extent, and there may be a purpose for these challenges.

Try to determine if there is a purpose or lesson. Offensive and difficult people could be in our lives to keep us continually reevaluating ourselves.

- Do we need to learn tolerance?
- Are we irritated because we know we need to reach out to them and help them in some way?
- Do we need to learn something about ourselves as reflected by their behavior?
- Are we being gracious, understanding, and compassionate with others?
- Are we being made uncomfortable to be pushed toward moving ourselves to a different place?
- Do we need to toughen up and learn to stand up for ourselves?
- Do we need to learn how to keep petty annoyances from distracting us?
- Do we need to figure out how to see God's love in people who are not so loveable?

Clearly, the only person I can change is myself; so I take responsibility to ensure each relationship is healthy and amiable, if at all possible. Trying to change the offensive or difficult person is a waste of time. They are who they choose to be. They can change, but you can't change them.

Some people are just irritating, but someone who is purposely making your life miserable is another story. While discussing this topic recently with a very wise man, he said it is important to speak up and to not let a person who is causing you anxiety upset your health. There is nothing noble about suffering in silence.

I was distraught about a work situation, and he said to not let it build. I had to get out of my comfort zone and tell someone to stop their offensive behavior towards me. It wasn't easy, but I did it, and things changed for the better.

When someone gets in your space, gets on your nerves, makes unwanted sexual comments, makes offensive comments, puts their hands on you, or shoots verbal jabs at you, you don't need to hold it inside. Speak up in a respectful, calm manner and describe to them how a specific behavior bothers or offends you. Some will be shocked because they didn't realize what they were doing, and they will make an effort to respect you. Some will not change because they are self-centered, insensitive clods. In that case, put it in God's hands and keep speaking up for yourself. Look for a way to stay away from them.

A former co-worker used to say, "Everyone brings joy to this office, some when they enter, and others when they leave." That's just the way life is, isn't it?

If there is a workplace problem and you are being harassed, evaluate whether escalation is needed. You have the right to work without being harassed. You may need to seek advice from a member of management or a professional counselor.

If you are "stuck" in an extremely bad or abusive situation, relationship, or job, continuing to be angry or hurt is a poor choice. You have choices. Make a better choice.

Evaluate if this is in your best interests and if it is what God wants for you. If it is not right, pray about it and look at options and alternatives. Ask yourself questions like these:

- Where is this career path taking me? Am I feeling anxiety about a job that isn't worth it? If it is a stressful or dead-end job, change your focus to finding a different job.

- Can I put up with an unpleasant supervisor or co-worker in exchange for this paycheck or should I look for another job?

  Note: Trying to get an employer or company to change is a waste of your time and energy. They are running their company exactly the way they want. Your decision is to stay, to go, or to find a way around the problem that is in your best interest. I got away from a bad boss by going back to school and getting a degree. With employment, you have options, although it might not always appear to be true.

  Important: I would not recommend walking out of a job until you find a different job.

- Is it worth it to continue in a line of work I hate, or can I use my free time to take classes toward another career path or to learn a different trade? Find out if the company has a tuition assistance program. Contact a school to see if there are grants available for you.

- Am I too old to change? Is it too late to make a major change in my life? When I lamented to my Dad that I was too old to go back to school, he asked, "How old will you be in four years when you get your degree?" Then he asked, "How old will you be in four years if you don't go after your degree?" His point was to go for it. Age is not a factor.

Family issues can be more difficult.

- Is it worth it to put up with an unpleasant, perhaps hateful in-law or can I do something to make things better? Should I turn the other cheek?

> *"...That ye resist not evil:*
> *but whosoever shall*
> *smite thee on thy right cheek,*
> *turn to him the other also."*
> Matthew 5:39

In this case, since the relative is part of your life, it would probably be wise to find a counselor who can help you discover a resolution to this conflict or ways to deal with this uncomfortable situation.

They love someone you love. It can be a very sensitive matter. Always treat them with love and respect, just as you would treat anyone.

> *"Love is the only force capable of*
> *transforming an enemy into a friend."*
> Martin Luther King, Jr.

- Should I let my spouse, boyfriend, or girlfriend hit me because I don't want to be divorced or alone? (That was a trick question. Get help now! No one deserves to be hit. Not ever!)

> If you are suffering stress and anxiety because someone is abusing you, hitting you, calling you names, and/or tormenting you,

relaxation techniques are not enough. You need a professional counselor to help you, and you need to take action right now.

Choices (a local support group for victims of domestic violence), teaches that the other person is making a choice to hurt you. That may be very difficult to hear. Yes, they are aware of what they are doing, and they are choosing to continue. Don't make excuses for them. Your choice is to continue to be hurt or to get help.

Call your local support group or call the National Domestic Violence Hotline at 1-800-799-7233.

Read "Codependent No More" or other books by Melody Beattie[x].

Seek professional counseling now.

Whether you are distressed about a work or family situation, do you believe it is what God wants for you? It is important to prayerfully evaluate your circumstances.

Intimidating People. It can be difficult and stressful dealing with professionals like doctors, attorneys, teachers, or government officials. You don't need to be intimidated. You are a grown up, and you have options that should be respected. You have the right to speak up and ask questions when you feel you are being forced or led into something that makes you uncomfortable or something that is not in your best interest. You have the right to ask about alternatives, side effects, options, ramifications, and documentation showing the success/failure data regarding their recommendation.

Change your perspective and think of them as your partners. They can be valuable resources.

I am always uncomfortable when visiting the doctor, but I used to be much worse. Several years ago I had an appointment with a doctor and I was very nervous about it until my friend Donna reminded me it's my body, and I have the right to make all the decisions. It reduced my stress tremendously. Dealing with extreme anxiety made me feel powerless. Once I realized my power, I could relax and face the appointment with more confidence. My healthcare provider became more of a resource and less a source of anxiety.

What my friend said made a lasting impact. When I had cancer, I had four "second opinions" until I was comfortable with my understanding of the diagnosis, the doctor, and the procedure. Would you be shocked to learn their professional opinions ranged from getting my affairs in order because I was going to die, to having radical surgery with a long recovery, to having an out-patient procedure with follow-up care to monitor the situation? Two of the four doctors recommended pretty much the same thing, so it reduced my anxiety to be able to go with their decision. The doctor I chose was great, and the procedure was successful. I thank God I got more than one professional opinion.

I'm *not* saying to refuse a recommendation because you don't want it or you are scared. I'm saying don't be intimidated by a professional or a diagnosis. Gather more information. Get a second, third, and fourth *professional* opinion. Learning you have choices can help you relax and focus on what you need to do. Sometimes we have to face procedures we really don't want. We do it anyway because it is for the best.

Find a doctor you can work with and one in which you have confidence.

Realize you have the right to speak up and ask questions, and you have the right to seek answers from more than one professional. It will reduce your anxiety.

Wrong Perspective. Use detached logic (like you are looking at the problem from the outside) to critically evaluate the situation and keep it in perspective.

If I am in a stressful situation, often I find myself horriblizing (churning the story in my mind and making it worse). When I notice that happening, I try to stop and logically and prayerfully evaluate what is going on. Reactions are often based on emotions, not logic, so it is helpful to try to separate the two. I verbalize or write out the cold, hard facts without any emotion and then I logically decide if my emotions are in proportion to the actual event. I might discuss the facts, not the emotions, with a friend or counselor to get some feedback.

Here are two scenarios where I can use logic to reduce or remove unnecessary stress and anxiety: (1) When I feel someone has offended me or (2) when I feel I have done something wrong.

In the first scenario, I take a step back and logically evaluate their intent. Are they unaware they have offended me? If this is the case, it is easier to let go of the emotional sting because that's life. Sometimes our feelings get hurt.

If the other person intentionally meant to hurt me, it can be a harder to let go of the anger. I find it puts up my defenses, and I don't want to feel that way. If it is possible to talk it out and clear the air, I try to do that. If they have a mental problem that makes them mean, it is beyond my control. Some people like to fight, and if you give them a target, they will take aim and the fight is on. When you don't make yourself a target, they will go find someone who will fight with them.

I don't have the time or energy to put up with folks who are mean, who try to provoke others into fighting with them, who love drama, or who make innuendos that sow discord. It makes sense to me to put them in God's hands and stay out of their way. I want to use my time and energy to enjoy my life.

"Don't let the negative few
influence the positive many."
Dr. Edward Cowgill

The second scenario makes me feel worse because I think I may have made a mistake or said or done something that offended another person. I'm surrounded by wonderful people and I don't want to hurt them so I can really beat up myself when I think I've done that. I've actually talked myself into panic attacks. I find the best thing to do is to ask forgiveness quickly. It can stop the pain. Most people will forgive, forget, and get on with life.

The tool here is to logically evaluate whether or not it is an appropriate reaction to feel stress or anxiety. Use logic to keep things in perspective.

Redirect Your Attention

When I focus on the cause of my anxiety, it increases. When I distract myself with something completely different, my anxiety is reduced.

When I experience anxiety over an event, I re-think it repeatedly. Do you do that too? It's like looking at it through a magnifying glass until in my mind, it becomes huge and distorted. Trying to not think of it doesn't work because the mind always thinks – you can't make it blank. It is more productive to focus on something to give your mind a break and change the direction of your thoughts.

Some of the things I do to redirect my attention have already been mentioned. Here are more.

Find an activity in which you can become totally absorbed. Here are some of my favorites that can take me emotionally and mentally to a better place.
- Read
- Get a change of scenery
- Start a hobby
- Take a class
- Meditate

Let's look at these one at a time.

Read. A wonderful way to relax is to become absorbed in a good book. Reading the right book can certainly inspire you to change your life.

> *"How many a man has dated a new era in his life*
> *from the reading of a book."*
> Henry David Thoreau

I usually read non-fiction. I like the real stuff. I want to learn about the successes of others. I want to be motivated. I'm drawn to self-help and inspirational books.

If you don't read very much, a good, inexpensive place to start is the public library or your church's library. Browse through any section that catches your attention.

This is not the time to choose a book someone said you should read about a topic that doesn't interest you. Go for something you think is exciting or interesting – something you can "sink your teeth into."

I go to the library and check out several books at once. I don't take out just one book because I want other choices if the first one doesn't hold my attention.

Some people can get completely swept away in a good novel and lose all track of time. They can become a hero, travel to exotic locations, solve mysteries, or have an exciting adventure all while sitting at home in a comfy chair.

Some people are the happiest when they are learning something. They use absolute concentration until they master a new skill or understand a difficult concept.

Other people want to drift away with beautiful poetry as the author uses words to weave a thought in a unique way.

If you have not read the Holy Bible, this is the perfect time. This can be the ultimate in relaxation. All those powerful scriptures and Bible stories can come to life for you.

"Till I come, give attendance to reading,
to exhortation, to doctrine."
1 Timothy 4:13

This is something you can do on your own, or there are probably active Bible study groups in your area. If this is of interest to you and you cannot find a group, why not start one? You don't need to be an expert; you only need to love the subject.

Reading the Bible strengthens faith, reduces anxiety, and gives direction. Read the Bible in a way that makes sense to you. Read it beginning to end, pick and choose different books of the Bible, start with the New Testament, or follow a study guide.

A study guide can provide more information and put things in context so they are easier to understand.

My Bible doesn't have a study guide, but it has a couple paragraphs of background before each book. For example, in Philippians, it tells me it was written by the Apostle Paul while he was in prison. It puts the letter with its message of joy and love in a different perspective than what I might have had otherwise.

I like to use my concordance to find what various scriptures say about a particular topic. A Bible concordance is a list of words from the Bible, arranged alphabetically, that cite where those words appear. For example, my concordance of the King James Version of the Holy Bible shows the word "glad" appearing 22 times in various passages. I can read each of those passages to get a deeper meaning for that word.

There is a lot of buzz right now about the law of attraction. There are several new books about it, but it's not a new concept. I heard my Dad talking about it thirty years ago. It's one of those things that just appears to be true. When you dwell on thoughts of past hurts, of negative experiences, and of fear about future events, you seem to pull more of that into your life. I don't understand it, but I've seen it happen in my life.

Let me put a Christian spin on the law of attraction: Read about, focus on, meditate on, and think about God and attract Him into your life.

Get a change of scenery. I work in a large office where the work is detailed, and I need to stay focused for too long. I find I do much better work and have less anxiety if I make it a point to get a change of scenery for a short time and think about something else. Even a few minutes can be refreshing.

Companies give workers break periods not because they want them to socialize and have fun, but because they want them to stay fresh and alert so they are more productive, they have fewer accidents, and they make fewer errors.

You can also take a break by going for a drive or walk with someone and not taking the problem with you. Talk about anything other than your problems.

Get out and get some fresh air.

Do something out of the ordinary. Some people get a break by having wild interests that might surprise you. I'm a pretty quiet and reserved person. I have a friend who is also pretty quiet and reserved. Would you believe we get season tickets to Ohio State University ice hockey and during games we can be seen in the front row, wearing our O.S.U. duds, yelling, cheering on the team, and beating on the glass? We have a blast. It's a great stress release. You can't think about your problems when you're eating cotton candy and laughing.

The point is to do something different and have fun. Do something that will cause you to focus in a completely different direction.

Today I am taking a break. I am exhausted, shaky, overworked, and about a minute away from tears. I enjoy my job and I don't like missing work, but today I just can't do it. I am in the middle of fixing up my home and there is so much work to do, but today I'm not going to lift one box or paint one wall or clean out one closet. Today I am taking a break. After breakfast, I am going to find a place to sit and read a book and enjoy doing nothing. My body and mind have hit their limit. The work, chores, clutter, and other people's needs will just have to wait. I need to take a real break.

So what did I do on my day off? After letting my supervisor know I would not be at work today, I turned off the alarm and slept in. I went to Cracker Barrel for lunch because I'm not cooking or washing dishes today. I went to the mall and returned a couple items. I didn't buy anything, but I had fun just strolling and seeing all the pretty things. I had a 20 minute back massage which helped my tense muscles. When I returned home, I got a favorite book and spent time in my hammock chair (Sky Chair[xi]) in the back yard, enjoying the fresh air and listening to the singing birds. Nice.

Start a Hobby. Is there something you have wanted to do but just haven't had the time or opportunity? Do it now. It can take your mind off your troubles and be a great stress reliever. Find a hobby that is different from what you normally do. For example, if you do paperwork and sit inside all day at your job, find a hobby or interest where you are outside and moving. If you are on your feet all day, find a hobby or interest where you can sit down and relax.

You can also look for a hobby group or club that sounds interesting to you. You can enjoy learning and socializing with like-minded people. Skill level doesn't matter. Joining a hobby group will get you out of the house so you will meet new people, which can help push your stress and anxiety to the background.

Take a Class. I'm always happy when I'm taking a class. It's helpful to me because I interact with others and feed off the group synergy. Being responsible for assignments with deadlines helps keep me focused. It's very relaxing to me because it redirects my attention away from my problems.

A school type of class is not for everyone, but there are many other types of classes. I've taken fun classes in knitting, basket weaving, piano, and guitar, to name a few.

Right now, I'm trying yoga for the first time and loving it. While I'm being a human pretzel, I can't think of other things.

It's always refreshing to try something new. It expands your world and builds your confidence.

Meditate. My approach to meditation is to think about a word, scripture, or concept from the Bible and see where it leads. When I meditate, my objective is to connect with God and welcome His guidance.

Many Christian people meditate. They focus on what is beneficial and positive. The Bible says to think on these things:

"Finally, brethren, whatsoever things are true,
whatsoever things are honest, whatsoever things are just,
whatsoever things are pure, whatsoever things are lovely,
whatsoever things are of good report, if there be any virtue,
and if there be any praise, think on these things."
Philippians 4:8

This can be a wonderful way to fill your mind with peaceful, comforting thoughts from the Word of God. Find passages that give you reassurance and meditate on their meaning. Focus on the topic without directing the mental conversation.

While meditating on a passage, you may find your mind wandering back to something negative. Gently redirect your focus back to the passage. Keep practicing; it will get easier.

Here are some Bible references about meditation:

"Blessed is the man [person] *that*
walketh not in the counsel of the ungodly,
nor standeth in the way of sinners,
nor sitteth in the seat of the scornful.
But his delight is in the law of the Lord,
and in his law doth he meditate day and night.
And he shall be like a tree planted by the river of water,
that bringeth forth his fruit in his season;
his leaf also shall not wither;
and whatsoever he doeth shall prosper."
Psalms 1:1-3

"I will meditate also of all thy work,
and talk of thy doings."
Psalms 77:12

"My meditation of him shall be sweet:
I will be glad in the Lord."
Psalm 104:34

Several things on which to meditate have already been mentioned. Here are more:

- Scripture
- The blessings you have received
- God's promises
- What heaven might be like
- The application of certain Bible lessons or stories
- Salvation
- Gratitude
- Forgiveness
- The love of God
- What has influenced you to lead a Christian life
- A memorable or recent sermon
- What is making a positive change in your life, your community, or your church
- What touches your heart and makes you smile

Find a topic in a concordance, read related scriptures, and then meditate and find the deeper lesson.

If while meditating a person comes to mind, pray for them then resume your meditation.

"Be still, and know that I am God:"
Psalms 46:10

Summary of Relaxation Tools from this Chapter

- Keep God's Words in your heart.

  o *"And to you who are troubled rest with us…"*
    2 Thessalonians 1:7

  o *"Come unto me, all ye that labour and are heavy laden,
    and I will give you rest." Matthew 11:28*

  o *"Six days shall work be done: but the seventh day is the
    Sabbath of rest, an holy convocation; ye shall do no work
    therein; it is the Sabbath of the Lord in all your
    dwellings." Leviticus 23:3*

  o *"Sing aloud unto God our strength: make a joyful noise
    unto the God of Jacob." Psalms 81:1*

  o *"The Lord is my strength and song…" Exodus 15:2*

  o *"…That ye resist not evil: but whosoever shall smite thee
    on thy right cheek, turn to him the other also."
    Matthew 5:39*

  o *"Till I come, give attendance to reading, to exhortation,
    to doctrine." 1 Timothy 4:13*

  o *"Finally, brethren, whatsoever things are true,
    whatsoever things are honest, whatsoever things are just,
    whatsoever things are pure, whatsoever things are lovely,
    whatsoever things are of good report, if there be any
    virtue, and if there be any praise, think on these things."
    Philippians 4:8*

  o *"Blessed is the man that walketh not in the counsel of the
    ungodly, nor standeth in the way of sinners, nor sitteth in
    the seat of the scornful. But his delight is in the law of the
    Lord, and in his law doth he meditate day and night. And
    he shall be like a tree planted by the river of water, that
    bringeth forth his fruit in his season; his leaf also shall*

not wither; and whatsoever he doeth shall prosper." Psalms 1:1-3

o "I will meditate also of all thy work, and talk of thy doings." Psalms 77:12

o "My meditation of him shall be sweet: I will be glad in the Lord." Psalm 104:34

o "Be still, and know that I am God" Psalms 46:10

- Let others inspire you.

o "Moderation in all things." (Andria Terence, Roman Comic Dramatist, (185 BC – 159 BC)

o "Love is the only force capable of transforming an enemy into a friend." Martin Luther King, Jr.

o "How many a man has dated a new era in his life from the reading of a book." Henry David Thoreau

o "Don't let the negative few influence the positive many." Dr. Edward Cowgill

- In the P.R.A.I.S.E. G.O.D. toolbelt, the letter R is for the tool "Relax."

- When you are experiencing anxiety or distress, praise God, pray, and then focus on relaxing your body.

- When you relax your body, you relax your mind. When you relax your mind, you relax your body. They are related. There is a connection.

- To reduce anxiety, relax your muscles, remove yourself from stressful situations, and/or redirect your attention.

- Use controlled breathing to calm your body.

- Try progressive relaxation to focus on relaxing one muscle group or area at a time. Visualize tension flowing out of your body as God's healing power flows in.

- Find out if a massage by a licensed massage therapist will work tension and soreness out of your muscles and help you feel better.

- Relax in a warm bath.

- Remove things in your life that make you feel anxious.

- Use a prioritized list to make sure you take care of the most important chores first.

- Schedule chores so you can have a day of rest every week.

- Decide if someone else can help with chores so you don't need to do everything yourself.

- Limit or avoid entertainment media that can be stressful.

- Limit contact with offensive or difficult people. Find a way to deal with them peacefully.

- Speak up if someone is behaving inappropriately towards you or harassing you. If he or she continues with bad behavior, seek advice from a professional counselor.

- Work as a partner with people in positions of authority and do not be intimidated. Remember you have the right to make choices and decisions for your life and your body. Gather information. Work as a team to reduce your anxiety level.

- Logically evaluate whether or not you should be feeling stress or anxiety. Use logic to keep things in perspective. Write out the cold, hard facts without any emotion and then logically decide if your emotions are in proportion to the actual event. You might discuss the facts, not the emotions, with a friend or counselor to get some feedback.

- Focusing on what is causing you to have anxiety is not always helpful. Sometimes you just need to get busy with something else. Think of an interesting way to divert your attention, such as reading. Read your Bible. Listen to audio books. Take a vacation. Take a walk to enjoy a change of scenery. Play a musical instrument. Start a hobby or take a class to learn a new skill. Do something fun that will make you laugh.

- Meditate on God's Word.

Tool #4
Attitude

PRAISE GOD™

PRAY
RELAX
ATTITUDE

The letter "A" in the P.R.A.I.S.E. G.O.D. toolbelt is for *Attitude*. There are three tools here.

- The first tool is the *Attitude of Gratitude*.

- The second tool is the *Attitude of Faith*.

- The third tool is the *Attitude of Forgiveness*.

An Attitude of Gratitude

> *"O give thanks unto the Lord; for he is good;*
> *for his mercy endureth for ever."*
> *1 Chronicles 16:34*

You might be thinking, "An attitude of gratitude? Are you kidding? I'm going through a horrible situation, my emotions are twisted, my world is coming apart, my heart is breaking, and you want me to be grateful?"

I'm not saying to deny those very real and deep feelings when bad things happen. And, I'm not saying to just snap out of it and move on. That's unreasonable. Most of us need time to process things, to understand the situation, to comprehend the impact, and to sort out our feelings.

We don't know why things happen the way they do. We simply don't have those answers.

The importance of this tool is to be in touch with God's healing, comforting power. Be willing to connect with your God in times of need and sorrow. Be open to gratefully accepting His help. You might find having an attitude of gratitude will help you feel better during this difficult time.

Recognize the support of good people and the encouraging influences in your life.

"In every thing give thanks: for this is
the will of God in Christ Jesus concerning you."
1 Thessalonians 5:18

When I worked at AT&T, I attended a seminar by the Lou Tice[xii] organization that included an exercise where I was asked to keep a stack of 3x5 cards with me and make note of anything I was grateful about. This struck a chord with me, and it opened my eyes to my many blessings. I was grateful for everything from the seminar facilitator, to the air conditioning, to the comfortable chairs, and so forth. After three days, I had listed hundreds of things. It changed my perspective.

I was even grateful for having note paper and a pen. Do you ever think about the people who wrote the Holy Bible? They didn't have those things. How did they ever accomplish so much without the writing tools we take for granted? It is easy to overlook all the amazing things we have today.

It just seems to me I have less stress and anxiety when I am looking for things for which I am grateful. It makes my day go better.

I read a story, I believe in one of Melody Beattie's[xiii] books, that tells about a woman who lived in a place that was not very nice. It was discouraging for her until she decided to change her way of thinking, be grateful for having her humble little home, and find what she could do to make it better. She fixed it up the best she could and it made a world of difference to her. She didn't have extra money to invest in expensive things, but the things she did were done with love and her perspective changed.

The exercise of giving thanks brings your mind into a closer relationship with God.

> *"Enter into his gates with thanksgiving,*
> *and into his courts with praise:*
> *be thankful unto him, and bless his name."*
> *Psalm 100:4*

Consider extending a word of gratitude to someone who has touched your life. Send a thank you note, send email, make a phone call, or thank someone face-to-face as the opportunity arises. Thank people who provide a service to you, such as waiters, waitresses, or clerks. It costs you nothing and it brightens someone else's day.

An Attitude of Faith

We can also get through difficult times by holding on to an attitude of faith.

> *"And Jesus answering saith unto them,*
> *Have faith in God."*
> *Mark 11:22*

An attitude of faith can be a challenge sometimes. I've had to continually use the tool of an attitude of faith to get through some of the big challenges in my life. It is good practice to develop an attitude of faith in small things, and you will be better prepared to use this tool when large things occur.

Having faith does not mean to be passive. Put a situation in God's hands then, take whatever action you can to ensure the needed outcome.

In prayer, we put problems or challenges in God's hands, but often we try to take back control or we don't ever actually let go of it completely. Is there a burden in your life you should release?

With sincere prayer and with an attitude of faith, you can let go and trust Him.

"If ye have faith as a grain of mustard seed,
ye shall say unto this mountain,
Remove hence to yonder place;
and it shall remove;
and nothing shall be impossible unto you."
Matthew 17:20

I recently had a small incident test my faith.

I live in Ohio, and we have some wicked winter storms. I work in an office about 45 minutes from my home. I was in the office at 6:00 in the evening when an ice storm hit. The county officials declared a winter weather emergency, meaning the roads were treacherous.

I was so focused on my work I was completely unaware of the winter storm until someone told me the roads were getting bad and to go home.

I left the office and after chipping about a quarter inch of ice off my car windows, I headed home. I could only drive about 20 to 30 miles an hour on the four-lane highway. The left lane was barely visible yet cars and semi trucks were passing me. I could not safely make it home, so I stopped at a hotel and got a room. As long as I was moving I was fine, but once I was in the room watching the non-stop news and weather reports on TV, my anxiety level went off the scale. I watched as they showed scenes of stranded motorists and wrecked cars. I was safe, but I watched the storm on TV for hours. I should have turned it off.

There was a tree outside my window that was covered with ice. If you haven't seen this kind of thing before, it is amazing. Rain falls and immediately freezes. Ice builds on each twig no matter how small. The glittering crystal trees are beautiful, but the extra weight can cause limbs to break and take down power lines. I could hear the snap of ice covered limbs breaking and crashing to the ground.

The TV reporters said the nearby town where I live was without power. I was afraid of what was happening at my home. My mind raced. Would my cat have enough food and water until I got home? Would the tree in the backyard fall on my house? Would the gas furnace continue to work? Would the pipes freeze? Was my insurance paid up? Would I be able to get home in the morning?

I couldn't sleep. I was safe, but I didn't feel safe. I felt alone and frightened. At about 2:30 a.m. the power in the hotel went out. Then I was lonelier and more anxious. My room was warm enough and I was fine, but I didn't feel that way. Where was my faith? The problem was clearly out of my control. I prayed but when I put it in God's hands, I didn't let go.

I sat and looked out the window for a couple more hours. I could occasionally see the lights of a vehicle creeping along the icy road. I called the hotel lobby, but no one answered. Had they left? I knew I was not completely alone because once in awhile I could hear someone in the hall.

Was I here at this place and time to have a moment to learn once again to lean upon the Savior? Perhaps.

I finally remembered to use my attitude of faith. I let go and was able to fall asleep.

Thankfully, the morning sun brought road crews clearing the way, the electrical power was restored, and all was well once more. However, it made me stop and re-examine my attitude of faith. I need to be faithful in ALL things. I had prayed, but I forgot to truly turn it over to God. It took me quite awhile to remember my attitude of faith.

A side note: At my home I had extra food and lots of supplies for just about every emergency – except for the emergency when I couldn't make it home. I think God was teaching me to have faith in Him, not my own resources.

When our faith is challenged, we can dig deeper into the Word of God and claim His promises. Adversity can bring a time of tremendous spiritual growth. The same old routine does not provide that kind of challenge. Be open to accepting you are a child of God, and you are in His hands. Ask Him, "What lesson is here?" It might not be apparent. Or, you may never know why something happened, but having faith means remembering:

"And we know that all things work together
for good to them that love God,
to them who are the called according to his purpose."
Romans 8:28

An Attitude of Forgiveness

Forgive Others. As in *The Lord's Prayer*, we are asked to forgive those who trespass against us. (Matthew 6:9-13 or Luke 11:2-4) That can be so hard. People do some very nasty things to other people. How can we forgive them?

"Forbearing one another,
and forgiving one another,
if any man have a quarrel against any;
even as Christ forgave you, so also do ye."
Colossians 3:13

I am in awe of Jesus' words from the cross:

"Father, forgive them;
for they know not what they do."
Luke 23:34

Jesus was asking God to forgive the people killing him! It makes me ashamed of my lack of forgiveness of others who do nothing more than verbally offend me.

Many times people don't comprehend the damage they are doing. From that perspective, it is a little easier to forgive.

Sometimes the abuse is intentional. Here is something I learned while dealing with someone who was particularly hurtful to me: She hurt me and walked away without a second thought. I continued to hold the hurtful incidents in my mind. As long as I was thinking about her, I felt injured. I would replay the many incidents in my mind and make myself sick to my stomach. Once I was able to forgive her (in my mind), I was at peace. I did not need to talk to her about what she had done.

Frankly, I think she enjoyed hurting me. I did not feel the need to tell her I forgave her. The negative energy was stuck in me. I needed to get rid of it for my sake. I choose to live in peace. Sometimes it's important to tell someone you forgive them, but I could not see the benefit in this particular case because it would promote further abuse.

Choices (a local support group for victims of domestic violence), teaches that when you tell an abusive person you forgive them and let them back into your life, it is giving them permission to hurt you again. This concept is so strange to me, but it is true. If an abusive person hits you and you forgive them and let them close to you again, they will hit you again. You don't need to take my word for this. Ask the professionals who deal with this all the time.

If you need help, call your local support group or call the National Domestic Violence Hotline at 1-800-799-7233, and they can help you find a support group in your area.

Recently I listened in amazement as a co-worker told and re-told a story of how someone had offended her. With each telling, the offense became more dreadful and the offending party more sinister. She didn't seem to realize what she was doing. She got herself extremely agitated, and I think she actually believed her own exaggerations. In addition to failing to forgive him, it got into the area of bearing false witness. If when the offense took place she would have graciously forgiven him, all that negativity would have disappeared.

Forgiving someone is something *you* do. They do not need to ask nor do they need to be "worthy" in your opinion.

When you think of forgiveness in terms of your own personal soul, peace of mind, and well-being, it makes sense to forgive. There is power in forgiveness. It has been my experience that letting go of a grudge or perceived offense can lower my heart rate and lower my blood pressure. Letting go may be the smartest move you can make for your own self. Replace anger with love for the benefits YOU receive.

"When you forgive,
you heal your own anger and hurt
and are able to let love lead again.
It's like spring cleaning for your heart."
Marci Shimoff [xiv]

Ask for Forgiveness. We have talked about us forgiving others, but there is also a need at times to ask others to forgive us. This can be difficult and very humbling. The best way to approach it is quick – like taking off a Band-Aid[TM] [xv]. When you mess up, don't wait. Ask for forgiveness and get it over with.

Forgive Yourself. How about forgiving yourself? I struggle with this. Most of us are harder on ourselves than we would ever be with another person. In my mind, I replay the stupid things I have said and done. Now that I know how un-forgiveness can harm me and forgiveness can radically change my life, I forgive myself. I ask for God's guidance and grace to help me improve.

If you are struggling with this, accept that everyone has flaws and making a mistake does not make someone a bad person.

Acknowledge your mistakes and resolve never to make that kind of mistake again. Try to find a way to move forward in a productive way.

Ask God for forgiveness. Do you feel you need forgiveness from God? Just ask Him.

"If we confess our sins, he is faithful and just
to forgive us our sins, and to cleanse us

from all unrighteousness."
1 John 1:9

With forgiveness, the big question is: do you want to stay in a place of resentment and hurt or do you want to get on with your life?

Summary of Attitude Tools from this Chapter

- Keep God's Words in your heart.

  o *"O give thanks unto the Lord; for he is good; for his mercy endureth for ever." 1 Chronicles 16:34*

  o *"In every thing give thanks: for this is the will of God in Christ Jesus concerning you." 1 Thessalonians 5:18*

  o *"Enter into his gates with thanksgiving, and into his courts with praise: be thankful unto him, and bless his name." Psalm 100:4*

  o *"Give thanks unto the Lord, call upon his name, make known his deeds among the people. Sing unto him, sing psalms unto him, talk ye of all his wondrous works. Glory ye in his holy name: let the heart of them rejoice that seek the Lord." 1 Chronicles 16:8-10*

  o *"And Jesus answering saith unto them, Have faith in God." Mark 11:22*

  o *"Now faith is the substance of things hoped for, the evidence of things not seen." Hebrews 11:1*

  o *"If ye have faith as a grain of mustard seed, ye shall say unto this mountain, Remove hence to yonder place; and it shall remove; and nothing shall be impossible unto you." Matthew 17:20*

- o *"And we know that all things work together for good to them that love God, to them who are the called according to his purpose."* Romans 8:28

- o *"Forbearing one another, and forgiving one another, if any man have a quarrel against any; even as Christ forgave you, so also do ye."* Colossians 3:13

- o *"Father, forgive them; for they know not what they do."* Luke 23:34

- o *"If we confess our sins, he is faithful and just to forgive us our sins, and to cleanse us from all unrighteousness."* 1 John 1:9

- Let others inspire you.

  - o *"If God didn't forgive sinners, Heaven would be empty."* Author unknown

  - o *"When you forgive, you heal your own anger and hurt and are able to let love lead again. It's like spring cleaning for your heart."* Marci Shimoff

  - o *Don't focus on the gap; focus on the good.*

- The "A" in the P.R.A.I.S.E. G.O.D. toolbelt represents Attitude.

- There are three tools here: An Attitude of Gratitude, an Attitude of Faith, and an Attitude of Forgiveness.

- Develop the habit of looking for good people and good things around you and giving thanks for your blessings. Yes, there are negative people and difficult situations but it is liberating to change your focus from negative to a positive attitude of gratitude.

- The exercise of giving thanks brings your mind into a closer relationship with God.

- Think of someone who has impacted your life in a positive, meaningful way and send them a thank you note or say a prayer of gratitude for them.

- Develop an attitude of faith in small things. When large events happen, you will be more prepared.

- Be open to accepting His help and comfort.

- Having an attitude of faith does not mean to be passive. When a problem is beyond your control, give it to God and let Him handle it, but you can continue to work toward the good outcome.

- When your faith is challenged, dig deeper into the Word of God and claim His promises.

- When your faith is challenged, ask Him to show you if there is a lesson here for you.

- Ask God to help you have an attitude of forgiveness.

- With Jesus as our example, we should forgive people who hurt us. Remember from the cross Jesus asked God to forgive the people who were torturing and killing him.

- Forgive others quickly. Ask for forgiveness quickly so bad feelings don't escalate.

- Forgiving someone is something *you* do. They do not need to ask nor do they need to be "worthy" in your opinion. Just forgive them.

- Forgive others to release yourself from the anger and hurt.

- Forgive yourself.

- Ask God for His forgiveness.

Tool #5
Inspiration

PRAISE | GOD ™

P R A I
R E T N
A L T S
Y A I P
X T I
U R
D A
E T
I
O
N

The letter "I" in P.R.A.I.S.E. G.O.D. stands for *Inspiration.*

In this section I would like to encourage you to evaluate the inspirational items and people surrounding you and see what else you can include to increase your emotional support.

An inspirational item, place, or person can remind you to redirect your thoughts from something stressful to something positive. We will look at:

- Inspiration at home
- Inspiration on the go
- Inspirational places
- Inspirational people

Surround yourself with inspirational people, places, and things because they help you focus on what is good and that pushes your troubles into the background.

Some days when life stinks, I want to retreat to my bedroom, lock the door, and never face the world again. After awhile I get bored, so I look around my room and see things that inspire me.

At the foot of my bed is a bookcase with my favorite books, videos, and CDs. Beside the bookcase are my framed certificates. They inspire me to not give up. The wall behind my bed is covered with pictures of family, friends, and ancestors. The photos show me that I am loved and there are people I love.

All these things motivate me to replace my feelings of anxiety with positive action or at least more constructive thoughts. They help me feel more secure and shift my attention in a better direction.

Remove negative items

Before we start adding things, let's get rid of items that have a negative feeling attached to them. Are there things in your home that make you feel bad or have negative memories attached to them? Do you have items that cause you to feel unhappy, guilty, or uneasy? Why are they in your home? I'm not talking about a rational or logical evaluation. This is about feeling. Inspiration is about feeling.

If you have a useful item but it holds a negative feeling or bad memory, someone else could use it. Pass the item on because it will not be a negative thing for another person. It might be a blessing to them. It doesn't matter if it has great monetary value. Your peace of mind is more valuable.

Many people have an item or heirloom that causes them to feel pain, anger, sadness, shame, or uneasiness. They justify keeping it because it belonged to a family member, it has some monetary value, or it represents family history so they think they can't throw it away. Give yourself permission to let it go.

A dear friend of mine suggested I take a picture to remember some items and then let them go. I did it and it was very freeing to not have the items cluttering up my home any longer.

I love my vintage Ethan Allen furniture. I used to have a cabinet with an upper shelf unit. One day I stumbled into it, and the upper part fell on me because it had not been attached properly. After that, I cringed every time I walked by it. The memory of it falling on me lingered. I sold it and got it out of the house. There wasn't anything wrong with it and I have purchased other matching pieces of furniture since then, but I could not live with something that made me uneasy.

Do you have jewelry from an old flame? When you look at it, do you feel sadness for a broken relationship? What is the point of keeping it? Even if it is an expensive item, if it makes you unhappy, get rid of it.

Well-meaning people can give you things that might not work out too well, but we hang on to them because they are gifts from friends.

For example, Mom had an operation and a friend sent her a lovely Christmas Cactus. It was a nice gift but it only bloomed on the anniversary of her surgery. We laughed about it on her anniversary, but it held the memory of a difficult time. No need to keep it.

What about the dirty dishes, laundry on the floor, stacks of clutter, things that need to be repaired, crafts that were never completed, and tasks left unfinished? When you see that, there is a negative pull. It can be subconscious, but it is still there. It creates negative feelings.

I have a clutter problem. I'll admit it. I have to set aside time to get the house back in order. It is usually a Saturday morning job. It's harder in the spring and summer when there is also yard work. I get embarrassed if someone stops by unannounced and the house is not tidy. When things are clean, I feel better and more relaxed.

I read a book by Karen Kingston called "Clear Your Clutter with Feng Shui."[xvi] It inspired me to be more organized. I don't follow or understand the beliefs and concepts of Feng Shui, but I completely understand the link between living in a clutter-free home and reduced stress and anxiety. The book had some good tips. Get rid of the clutter to let in light and to let fresh air circulate.

When my surroundings are in order, I feel more in control and better able to handle anxiety and stress.

Inspiration at Home

Have you ever gone into a church or cathedral and spent time looking at the magnificent religious paintings, stained glass windows, statues, and objects? Some depict the life of Christ, the crucifixion, or the glory of God. They are not there by accident. They are there to touch our hearts, to remind us of the wonders of our God, and to strengthen our faith. They are intended to inspire and motivate us.

Use that same objective to surround yourself with items in your home.

It is worthwhile to take some time to examine each room of your home. Look at the items you have chosen to hang on the walls or place on shelves. Evaluate the items being displayed and being used. Some things are neutral, but others have strong emotional attachments.

I purposely surround myself with things I love. My pictures, books, and treasures make me smile. I have family portraits. I have a large picture of Jesus, which was in our home while I was growing up. Before that, it hung in my Mom's home when she was growing up.

My bookshelf includes works by Robert Schuller[xvii], Og Mandino[xviii], and a book my mother wrote called "Edward and Me[xix]." I also have a Dr. Seuss[xx] book called "Oh the Places You Will Go" that was read by Dr. Otte[xxi] at my graduation ceremony from Franklin University.

It's mid-January but the nativity set is still on my mantle because I just love it and I'm not ready to pack it away.

I also have a clock that was given to me to commemorate my many years of service with AT&T.

On vacation many years ago, my parents and I walked on the beach in Florida and picked up seashells that I brought home and put in a frame. I treasure it because of the memory. There is no monetary value, but it makes me smile so it is displayed in my home.

I surround myself with things I love. These items are not necessarily financially valuable, but they make me happy. They inspire me to stay strong and to keep moving forward with my desires and goals, and not let anxiety and fear hold me back.

Do you have things in drawers or hidden in closets that have meaning to you but they are not where you can see them? Consider displaying them.

My Bible is visible but it doesn't have a permanent spot. It travels with me from room to room as needed.

Is your Bible tucked away in a drawer, or is it on the counter with signs of wear, marks, dog-eared, and tear-stained? Go ahead and wear it out. If you need to keep the family Bible in perfect condition, that's okay. Put it somewhere safe and go out and get a working copy you can mark up and use until it falls apart.

My previous home had much of the same contents as this one, but the home itself had a lot of bad memories and I had to move.

Place inspirational items around your home that make you feel good and motivate you to take actions to achieve the desires of your heart.

Inspiration on the Go

This project is always on my mind. Wherever I look, I get inspiration for new things I can create and innovative ways to get my tools and toolbelt to people who can benefit from them. It seems every store has something that gets me fired up to rush home so I can work on a new companion piece. The world is full of inspiration!

Booklets. I like to have little booklets with me for inspiration just in case I need to wait somewhere. I find it's easier to pass the time if I have something to hold my attention.

In my tote bag right now is a little book about angels. It's just the right size to fit in a side pocket.

There used to be little booklets at the checkout counter in the grocery, but I haven't seen any in awhile. I still have some. I have one in my desk at work that describes what the Bible says about being happy.

When I browse the bookstore, I often find just the perfect inspirational booklet to add to my supply.

I have created little booklets about this program to fit in the toolbelt. They can help you remember the tools for handling stress while you are on the go. They don't contain all the content from the book. They are meant to be notes to reawaken your mind to what you have learned.

Pop a booklet in your pocket, handbag, backpack, laptop case, briefcase, glove compartment, book bag, or the baby's travel bag so it's handy when you need it.

Radio and CD Player. If the news on the car radio is causing you anxiety about the state of the world, find a Christian radio station that shares the Good News. I find I can literally, change my feelings with the push of a button.

For an inspirational boost while driving, I have CDs of my favorite artists in my car.

When the radio and CDs are not inspiring me, I sing a favorite song, or gospel tune. You can do that too. When you have kids in the car, teach them your favorite song so you can all sing together.

Pictures. Keep pictures of loved ones in your wallet to inspire you and help you keep things in perspective.

Jewelry. Often someone wearing a lovely cross will catch my attention. This works two ways. It inspires them because they know they are wearing it, and it inspires others who see it. Pretty cool.

Have you ever noticed how many people wear angel pins? If you have one, don't leave it at home in a drawer. Wear it proudly.

Do you have a locket with a picture of someone you love? You don't have to wait for a special occasion. Make every day special and wear it all the time.

If your spouse or another loved one has given you a piece of jewelry, you can wear it to be reminded of how much they care for you. Treasured gifts from loved ones can inspire us to stay strong for one another.

Daily Reading. Many people start or end their day with an inspirational reading. This is a great idea. Rather than jump out of bed and race to get ready for work, it's a better idea to spend a moment with God and thank Him for another day. I have a calendar with something inspiring to think about every day. Consider this: Get a calendar with daily inspiration, read the page and then rip it out and take it with you to refer to again later in the day.

Religious Items. In my handbag, I usually have a prayer book or other inspirational item. It gives me a reminder to ask for help when needed. I don't ever want to be at a hospital or other critical scene without something to immediately remind me to keep in touch with God and ask for His help.

Some people carry religious metals, prayer cards, or prayer cloths.

At Work. On my desk at work I have a little plastic Nativity scene less than 2 inches high that I put up last Christmas and plan to leave up. It is so small few people notice it. I notice it. That's my point. I have things that bring me joy and/or inspire me and help me keep my mind on Jesus.

These are things that can take the energy away from a negative punch and keep us focused on what is important.

"Thou wilt keep him in perfect peace,
whose mind is stayed on thee: because he trusteth in thee.
Trust ye in the Lord for ever:
for in the Lord JEHOVAH is everlasting strength."
Isaiah 26:3-4

Inspirational Places

An inspirational place (or place of solitude) can draw your thoughts away from whatever is causing you distress and toward something positive. Do you have a place that inspires you? It can be a place you love to visit to relax, to feel at peace, and to get recharged. A few times I have sat quietly in an empty church just to absorb the peace and love of a Holy place where God's people gather to worship Him.

Places like art galleries, craft shows, or hobby shops inspire me to try my hand at creating something fun or artistic.

If you have not thought about a place you can visit for inspiration, consider doing so. It can be a fascinating museum, a bookstore, the library, an unusual or historic location, a park, a nearby coffee shop, or a vacation destination.

For some people, home is neither safe nor peaceful, so it helps to find a safe haven elsewhere for inspiration. The structure doesn't matter; it's the feeling you get when you are there. A place where you feel secure can reduce your anxiety.

When you can't physically be in a safe, peaceful, inspirational place, you can go there mentally and draw on the memory to get the same serene feeling. Have you ever been talking to someone and they say something like, "When I was a child...," or "Once on vacation...," or "When I lived in...," and they get a faraway look in their eyes? They are reliving a fond memory. Do that!

The place can be somewhere you visited, or you can create an ideal place in your mind. The technique is the same. Mentally put yourself somewhere that redirects your thoughts and focus, which will help you get through the latest challenge. It can help you think about what you want for your life and perhaps inspire you to take action. If you can't go there physically, you can always close your eyes for a few minutes and go there in your mind.

Inspirational People

Once in awhile someone will cross your path who will profoundly change your life.

"There are two things that will change your life:
The books you read and the people you meet."
Author unknown

Seek out and begin a friendship with people who inspire you. Do you know a church leader, community leader, or someone else who you feel has a dynamic message or is doing amazing work? Is there someone you think is on the right track? Give them a call or send an email or letter and ask if you can buy them lunch or a cup of coffee. What could it hurt? They may say, "Yes." Ask them about their walk, mission, job, or volunteer work, as appropriate. Talk about what they are doing that you think is impressive. They are probably passionate about their work and eager to share information.

When we talk to people who are passionate, it inspires us.

Enjoy the synergy of Christian fellowship.

> *"For where two or three*
> *are gathered together in my name,*
> *there am I in the midst of them."*
> *Matthew 18:20*

Seek out a group whose members are passionate about God and His work. Get inspired and get involved.

Likewise, authors write books that can excite us to new ways of thinking and inspire our personal growth. They can stir us into action. Find authors you like and send letters or emails and tell them what in their work inspired you. It might lead to an awesome friendship.

A friend of mine wrote a fan letter to her favorite author, and the author responded with an invitation to hear her speak at a conference. I got to go too. It was a delightful experience.

Authors and inspirational speakers travel throughout the country for book signings and presentations. Watch for them to visit your area. It can be a real treat to see them in person.

I don't understand people who don't go to church or listen to ministers of the Word. There is so much inspiration, motivation, and support available. If one church or speaker doesn't touch your heart, keep searching.

"...seek, and ye shall find..."
Matthew 7:7

"...seek, and ye shall find..."
Luke 11:9

It's in there twice. It must be true.

Summary of Inspirational Tools from this Chapter

- Keep God's Words in your heart.

  o *"Thou wilt keep him in perfect peace, whose mind is stayed on thee: because he trusteth in thee. Trust ye in the Lord for ever: for in the Lord JEHOVAH is everlasting strength." Isaiah 26:3-4*

  o *"For where two or three are gathered together in my name, there am I in the midst of them." Matthew 18:20*

  o *"...seek, and ye shall find..." Matthew 7:7*
  "...seek, and ye shall find..." Luke 11:9

- Let others inspire you.

  o *"There are two things that will change your life: The books you read and the people you meet."* Author unknown

- The letter "I" in the P.R.A.I.S.E. G.O.D. toolbelt is to remind us to surround ourselves with inspiration.

- Before you add inspirational items to your surroundings, remove items from your life that hold a negative or bad feeling. Inspiration is about feeling. Get rid of anything that makes you feel bad.

- Clutter reminds you consciously or subconsciously, you need to get rid of the mess and chaos. Get rid of clutter to let in light and to allow fresh air to circulate. Donate extra items so other people can use them.

- Unfinished projects weigh on your mind, sometimes for years. Finish projects, get rid of any unfinished projects, or hire someone else to complete the project for you.

- After negative things, things that hold bad feelings, and things that make you sad have been removed from your home, evaluate if you are now surrounded with things you love, things that give you a feeling of peace, things that inspire you to have a closer walk with God, and things that inspire you to do something positive. Inspirational things help you focus on what is good, which pushes your troubles into the background.

- The logical side of your mind tells you to do a particular activity, but it is the feeling side that motivates you to take action. Look for things that inspire and motivate you in a positive direction.

- Have inspirational items in your home. Surround yourself with things you love, that inspire you, that touch your heart, and make you smile.

- Do you have items, treasures, and keepsakes in drawers, boxes, or closets that have comforting or inspiring feelings attached to them? Get them out where you can see them.

- Keep a working Bible in sight all the time and refer to it often. Wear it out.

- When traveling, set your car radio to a Christian radio station or keep CDs in the car in case you need an inspirational boost.

- Find inspirational little booklets you can take with you when you leave home. You never know when you will have time on your hands and need some inspiration to stay strong.

- Get a calendar with inspirational daily readings you can tear out and carry with you each day.

- Visit inspirational places.

- Attend weekly worship services to get an inspirational lift.

- Seek out friends who inspire you in a positive direction.

- Ask a church leader what books and authors they like and what inspires them.

- See if your Christian bookstore has book signings or readings. Make it a point to attend and meet the authors in person.

- Attend presentations by inspirational speakers.

- Watch inspirational people on TV.

- When something or someone inspires you to do something, take action.

Tool #5 Inspiration

Tool #6
Self-Talk

| P | R | A | I | S | E | — | G | O | D | ™ |

PRAY
RELAX
ATTITUDE
INSPIRATION
SELF TALK

In the P.R.A.I.S.E. G.O.D. toolbelt, the letter "S" stands for *Self-Talk[xxii]*. Self-talk is that constant chatter that goes on in your head.

The reason self-talk is a stress management tool is because you can learn to manage the negative chatter. Let's look at self-talk and how to:

- Become aware of your self-talk
- Observe what you say to yourself
- Create and apply new messages
- Learn more about self-talk

The P.R.A.I.S.E. G.O.D. toolbelt is not a hobby; it is my life. I use these tools every day. I could not be more serious about this. The tools in this toolbelt have practical, real-life application.

I just went through a stressful situation this evening – one most people would not necessarily see as stressful. But I'm sitting here replaying the event in my mind. The self-talk inside my head is telling me "I'm stupid, stupid, stupid. I said the wrong thing. I did the wrong thing. I am such an idiot." That is what negative self-talk does: It beats us up. We beat up ourselves.

In my case, my heart starts racing and my negative thoughts fly as relatively insignificant events become unbearable. If you have had this kind of anxiety, obsession, or panic attack, you know it can be miserable.

Self-talk is what you say to yourself about yourself, other people, situations, events, conversations, circumstances, conditions, and so forth. Negative, judgmental chatter increases your stress level. For those who suffer from stress, anxiety, and worry, an overload of negative self-talk can be incapacitating. I have gotten to that point. Now I use the tools to calm negative self-talk and get back on track.

Become Aware of Your Self-Talk

You may have seen the cartoon with a little devil whispering in one ear and a little angel whispering in the other. The debate is self-talk.

You can't turn off the chatter in your head. It's always there. Usually, my self-talk is just random chatter and observations. What thoughts are going through your head unchecked? Start becoming aware.

You can rewrite those messages.

Did you just think, "No, I can't" or "Yippee, teach me how" or something else? That is your self-talk. The first step is to become aware the messages are ever present.

Observe What You Say to Yourself

Do you realize many of us say terrible things to our own sweet, precious souls we would never say to another person? Be nice to yourself. Talk to yourself the way you would talk to a best friend or other loved one.

"But I say unto you,
that every idle word that men shall speak,
they shall give account thereof in the day of judgment."
Matthew 12:36

Does this include words we say to ourselves?

Here is an interesting exercise. Over the next few days, notice the things you say to yourself and take notes. The results can be enlightening.

What are you telling yourself? Is the chatter judgmental, self-limiting, or negative? Think about the impact.

Are your words judgmental of others?
- How could she wear that?
- That guy is an idiot.
- She is so messy.
- How could he go out in public looking like that?
- She looks like a tramp.
- He looks like one of "them."
- He's a liar.
- The management here is incompetent.

Are your words self-limiting?
- I can't do that.
- I'm afraid to _____ because something bad will happen, or I will look stupid and people will laugh at me.
- I can't sleep.
- I'm not smart enough.
- No one likes me.
- I'm too old to learn something new.
- I can't talk in front of a crowd.
- I'll never get this done.
- I can't handle this.

Is the chatter in your head negative?
- I can't get a job because the economy is terrible.
- People are just mean.
- This will never work.
- The government doesn't care about us. We're doomed.
- It's too hot, cold, rainy, dry, or windy.

Observe your self-talk for a few days and see if a pattern emerges.

Is there chatter in your head that repeats something hurtful a parent, a spouse, a teacher, or someone else said to you? Just because an authority figure said something, does not make it true. Sometimes we carry those painful words with us for many years or maybe even a lifetime.

Do you replay an argument in your mind and think of what you will say next time? Have you been preparing for an argument and waiting for the opportunity to tell someone a well-rehearsed slam?

Why are you saying these things to yourself? I find even a little negative self-talk if left unchecked, can grow and wear you down. It can be very destructive. It's time to let go.

The more I overload myself with judgmental, self-limiting, and negative thoughts, the more of that I see in the world and the more I experience judgment and hostility from others. I wonder if this is one aspect of *"Judge not, that ye be not judged"* (Matthew 7:1) because it seems to have a boomerang effect.

> *"What you see in the world sees you."*
> Dr. Edward Cowgill

Norman Vincent Peale recognized the same reaction from others as mentioned in his book, "The Positive Power of Jesus Christ." He talks about having an inferiority complex when he was young and found "people will unconsciously take you at your own self-appraisal." [xxiii] Norman's father was a minister, and they prayed God would correct the "unhealthy thought pattern."

It is time to pray God will correct any unhealthy thought patterns that are harming you and replace them with messages in harmony with God's Word.

Create and Apply New Messages

Now that you have identified some self-talk that might be contributing to your stress level, let's look at ways to turn it around and stop the "stinkin' thinkin'," [xxiv] as Charlie "Tremendous" Jones used to say.

> *"...let the weak say, I am strong."*
> *Joel 3:10*

Follow these steps to create powerful, positive self-talk messages.

1. Pick out one troubling judgmental, self-limiting, or negative self-talk message you say to yourself.

2. Write out a positive, loving message you can use as a substitute.

    a. **Write** out the new message on paper. Don't just do this part of the task in your head.

    b. Use the present tense.

    c. Use strong words.

    d. Create a message that is short and easy to remember.

    e. Make sure the message is in accord with Bible teachings.

    f. Repeat the positive message several times to be sure you are comfortable with the wording.

3. When you start thinking an old message, quickly and firmly replace it with your new positive message. Let the

negative message trigger the positive message so this becomes an automatic response.

When I reviewed my self-talk, I was able to identify certain destructive thought patterns. Then I created kind, helpful, gentle, loving, uplifting messages to counteract them. You can do the same.

Just as mentioned in the section about guided relaxation, wording is important.

Don't say, "I am not stupid." (negative)
Say, "I am learning more all the time!" (positive)

Don't say, "I'm not unattractive." (negative)
Say, "I am attractive!" (positive)

Messages like "I am getting smarter" or "I'm learning more all the time," or "I forgive quickly," move you forward in a positive direction. Positive statements make you feel confident.

Use exclamation points. Make the messages strong. Using strong emotion makes the statement more powerful.

Negative self-talk is usually over the top. Make the counteractive statements over the top as well. Say, "I'm attractive" and mean it!

Statements like "I'm so stupid" can make you feel defeated and worthless. I actually get a physical feeling of withdrawal when I just read it.

If you make a mistake, it is a learning experience, not a fatal error. Stop replaying it in your mind by creating and applying positive self-talk. Choose to not participate in self-defeating talk.

Some people might argue that thinking differently is too small a solution to combat some of the tremendous struggles we face. Some might try positive thinking for a short time, and if they don't see the results they want immediately, they go back to their old patterns. Some might be put off by a suggestion to use "positive thinking," but it has become a cliché because *it works.*

Break the Habit. Negative self-talk is a habit and habits can be broken.

Steps to break a bad habit:

1.   Recognize you have a bad habit and be willing to do what it takes to change.

2.   Replace the bad habit with a good habit.

3.   Reward yourself when you do well and forgive yourself if you slip up.

4.   Repeat as needed.

More About Self-Talk

Memorize Scripture. You can replace judgmental, self-limiting, and negative self-talk with memorized scripture. When your head is full of racing self-talk, start focusing on those scriptures.

Judgmental Self-Talk. Quite simply, people are going to catch our attention if they look or behave differently than we would expect. The thing to remember about these folks is that we are told to not judge.

> *"Judge not, that ye be not judged."*
> *Matthew 7:1*

We don't know their hearts. We don't know their paths. What we can do is treat them with courtesy and respect, pray for them, and when the opportunity arises, share our faith with them.

> *"...for the Lord seeth not as man seeth;*
> *for man looketh on the outward appearance,*
> *but the Lord looketh on the heart."*
> *1 Samuel 16:7*

<u>Self-Limiting Self-Talk</u>. Avoid giving yourself self-limiting messages. Let God's Word empower you.

If you think, "I can't do this." Replace it with:

> *"I can do all things through Christ*
> *which strengtheneth me."*
> *Philippians 4:13*

If you think, "They are out to hurt me or discredit me." Replace it with:

> *"If God be for us, who can be against us?"*
> *Romans 8:31*

If you are afraid, think:

> *"For God hath not given us the spirit of fear;*
> *but of power, and of love, and of a sound mind."*
> *II Timothy 1:7*

> *"In God have I put my trust.*
> *I will not be afraid what man can do unto me."*
> *Psalm 56:11*

You can humbly submit yourself to God's will and let Him guide your steps.

> *"Trust in the Lord with all thine heart;*
> *and lean not unto thine own understanding,*
> *In all thy ways acknowledge him,*
> *and he shall direct thy paths."*
> *Proverbs 3:5-6*

There is no need for a child of God to think less of himself or herself.

> *"Ye are of God, little children,*
> *and have overcome them;*
> *because greater is he that is in you,*
> *than he that is in the world."*
> *1 John 4:4*

You are not on this journey alone.

> *"...I am not alone, because the Father is with me."*
> *John 16:32*

Negative self-talk. Negative self-talk is not productive. If you see something is not right, perhaps God is opening your eyes to a problem you need to help correct. "God so loved the world that he gave his only begotten son." How could that be interpreted to mean negative talk about the world is acceptable? That scripture tells me I also have the responsibility to love the world and work to make it a better place.

> *"For God so loved the world*
> *that he gave his only begotten Son,*
> *that whosoever believeth in him should not perish,*
> *but have everlasting life."*
> *John 3:16*

Let's look at some of the negative self-talk examples listed previously.

- I can't get a job because the economy is terrible.

  - Perhaps you should think about how you can improve your financial situation by focusing on how you can work for God. *("The harvest truly is plenteous, but the labourers are few." Matthew 9:37)* He will supply your needs. *("But my God shall supply all your needs according to his riches in glory by Christ Jesus." Philippians 4:19)*

- Perhaps you should learn how to start your own business to participate in energizing the economy.

- Look for a job-seekers networking group in your church or in other churches.

- People are just mean.
  - If you think, "People are just mean," you know that broad generalization is just not true. Associate with other people. There are about 7 billion to choose from, 33% of whom are Christians.[xxv]

  - We are surrounded by loving, genuinely kind-hearted people. They are in service organizations, health care fields, and in religious groups. Good people volunteer at schools, homeless shelters, and food banks. They are also in your neighborhood, church, supermarket, and place of employment. Reach out and get to know some of the wonderful people around you.

- This will never work.
  - Give it a try. What is the point of claiming defeat before the battle?

- The government doesn't care about us. We're doomed.
  - Run for office and fix it!

- It's too hot, cold, rainy, dry, or windy.

  - Too hot? Take it easy and drink lots of water.

  - Too cold? Get a blanket and snuggle with your sweetheart.

  - Too rainy? Get an umbrella and go out singing in the rain.

  - Too dry? Go swimming or run through the sprinkler.

- Too windy? Buy or make a kite and teach a child how to fly it. Make a happy memory for both of you.

Words change things. This includes the words we say to ourselves. Don't ever underestimate the power of your words. Choose them carefully.

> *"Let the words of my mouth,*
> *and the meditation of my heart,*
> *be acceptable in thy sight,*
> *O Lord, my strength, and my redeemer."*
> *Psalm 19:14*

<u>Evidence</u>. Display things that are evidence of your value and accomplishments to inspire and support your positive self-talk.

When negative self-talk tells me I'm stupid, I look at my certificates that I have framed and hanging on my bedroom wall. It stops the negative self-talk because I have evidence I can learn anything I choose. I would highly recommend displaying evidence of your accomplishments, whatever that means to you.

Raising a child is tremendously important work. I display treasures that hold happy memories of raising my child.

Many people display trophies, their artwork, their needlework, and so forth, that shows what they have accomplished. This practice can help influence positive self-talk.

Use Purposeful, Powerful, Positive Self-Talk. No one has the power to control your self-talk, only you. Use self-talk to manage stress and anxiety.

Self-talk can be used to calm your nerves. We don't always have another person right there to help us, but God is always there. Use self-talk and also talk to God. Let the peace that surpasses all understanding surround you, fill your heart, fill your mind, and lift you up to face the challenges of the moment.

"And the peace of God,
which passeth all understanding,
shall keep your hearts and minds
through Christ Jesus."
Philippians 4:7

Believe. It is important you believe your new self-talk statements you now say to yourself to counteract the old messages. If you are having trouble going forward with this tool, keep working on creating self-talk statements that are positive, loving, and *believable* for you.

"For as he thinketh in his heart, so is he"
Proverbs 23:7

This tool is most useful if you do the recommended exercise. If you have not done it yet, you can do it now. Here are the steps again.

1. Observe your self-talk for a few days. Examine those messages and see if you can find trends or if you can identify the most frequent destructive ones.

2. Create (write out) positive messages as described previously that counteract the negative ones.

3. Practice counteracting harmful self-talk with strong positive self-talk.

Summary of Self-Talk Tools from this Chapter

- Keep God's Words in your heart.

  o *"But I say unto you, that every idle word that men shall speak, they shall give account thereof in the day of judgment." Matthew 12:36*

  o *"...let the weak say, I am strong." Joel 3:10*

  o *"Judge not, that ye be not judged." Matthew 7:1*

  o *"...for the Lord seeth not as man seeth; for man looketh on the outward appearance, but the Lord looketh on the heart." 1 Samuel 16:7*

  o *"I can do all things through Christ which strengtheneth me." Philippians 4:13*

  o *"If God be for us, who can be against us?" Romans 8:31*

  o *"For God hath not given us the spirit of fear; but of power, and of love, and of a sound mind." II Timothy 1:7*

  o *"In God have I put my trust. I will not be afraid what man can do unto me." Psalm 56:11*

  o *"Trust in the Lord with all thine heart; and lean not unto thine own understanding, In all thy ways acknowledge him, and he shall direct thy paths." Proverbs 3:5-6*

  o *"Ye are of God, little children, and have overcome them; because greater is he that is in you, than he that is in the world." 1 John 4:4*

  o *"...I am not alone, because the Father is with me." John 16:32*

  o *"For God so loved the world that he gave his only begotten Son, that whosoever believeth in him should not perish, but have everlasting life." John 3:16*

- o *"The harvest truly is plenteous, but the labourers are few."* Matthew 9:37

- o *"But my God shall supply all your needs according to his riches in glory by Christ Jesus."* Philippians 4:19

- o *"Let the words of my mouth, and the meditation of my heart, be acceptable in thy sight, O Lord, my strength, and my redeemer."* Psalm 19:14

- o *"And the peace of God, which passeth all understanding, shall keep your hearts and minds through Christ Jesus."* Philippians 4:7

- o *"For as he thinketh in his heart, so is he"* Proverbs 23:7

- Let others inspire you.

  - o *"What you see in the world sees you."* Dr. Edward Cowgill

  - o *"Stop the stinkin' thinkin'."* Charlie "Tremendous" Jones

- In the P.R.A.I.<u>S</u>.E. G.O.D. toolbelt, the letter "S" reminds us to use positive self-talk.

- Understand there is self-talk going on in your head all the time, and you can control it.

- Replace negative, judgmental, or limiting self-talk with positive, loving, and empowering self-talk.

- For each troubling, negative self-talk message, create and memorize a positive, believable message you can use each time the negative message crosses your mind. The negative self-talk now triggers your use of the positive message that counteracts the negative one.

- Sometimes limiting self-talk comes from something hurtful said to you many years ago. In your heart, forgive the person who said it. That comment is not true. It's time to let it go from your mind.

- Be nice to yourself. Talk to yourself the way you talk to a dear friend.

- Deal with reality and don't let negative self-talk cause you to overreact.

- Negative self-talk is a habit and habits can be broken.

- Design your self-talk so it is in synchronization with the messages in the Bible.

- Memorize scripture that will counteract negative self-talk and fear.

- Carefully choose words you say to yourself. Don't underestimate the power of your self-talk messages.

- Use purposeful, powerful, positive self-talk to manage stress and anxiety.

- Redirect your self-talk to talking with Jesus.

Tool #7
ENERGIZE!

PRAISE — GOD ™

P R A I S E
P R A I S E
R E T N E N
A L T S L E
Y A I P F R
  X T I   G
    U R T I
    D A A Z
    E T L E
      I K
      O
      N

The "E" in the P.R.A.I.S.E. G.O.D. toolbelt stands for *Energize*!

When we are under stress, it's easy to forget our physical needs. It's important to keep our bodies healthy and functioning properly so we are better prepared to physically manage stress and anxiety and to get rid of the excess stress-related chemicals.

The focus of this section is making lifestyle changes to move towards getting in better shape. Even small changes can have big benefits.

If you enjoy workouts, running, weight training, and/or a healthful diet, excellent! Continue what you are doing to reap the rewards of being active and healthy.

I know I always feel better when I stick to a program or plan that improves my health. Focus on becoming energized so you can feel better too.

Here are some things I have learned: To feel better, get some regular physical activity and have a healthful diet. Okay, so it isn't earth shaking news. You already know it. Let's look at some information anyway. There may be something here that inspires you to take an action step toward better health.

Exercise Regularly

Important: Before starting any exercise program, consult your doctor or healthcare professional to make sure the exercise you have in mind is safe for you.

Who wants to exercise? Not me.
Who wants to feel better? I do.
I see a conflict here.

Let's look at this from a practical point of view. The body is designed to move, and you are more likely to exercise if you find an activity you enjoy. It can be anything, such as taking an exercise class, walking, learning to line dance, dancing with your sweetheart, or working in a garden. Find an activity you enjoy, decide on a schedule, and make a commitment.

During times of excess stress, the body gets a rush of stress-related chemicals. We get the same rush our ancestors did to help them when running from dangerous animals or battling enemies. If we find our life is not in danger, our bodies still have all those unneeded chemicals. When the body is in good shape, it can recover quickly. If not, you might continue to have panic and anxiety feelings for hours afterward because of those chemicals. I have experienced prolonged sweating, racing heart, jittery nerves, and so forth.

When feeling anxious or stressed, some people want to sit down and try to calm their nerves. Others need to get up and move. I'm a get up and move kind of person. I usually walk until I'm exhausted. It helps.

There are many reasons to make a concerted effort to start or increase a program of regular physical activity. Just feeling better is a pretty good one. It's a choice. Make a choice to feel better and be healthier.

Start any new effort with good information and prayer.

Options. There are lots of options for exercising.

If there is a gym, YMCA, or another kind of fitness center in your area, it can be a tremendous resource. Stop by and talk to a trainer about their different classes and activities.

Some hospitals provide low-cost fitness programs. You can enjoy the company of others while getting instructions from professionals.

There are also lots of sports teams and leagues in most areas. Joining a group or team is a healthy social outlet and it holds you responsible for participating and doing your part.

I've learned some inexpensive alternatives, such as walking in the neighborhood or walking at the mall. I know this sounds pretty tame, but it works for me.

Our mall has distance markers on the wall so you can see how far you have walked. They open the doors at 6:30 a.m. for walkers while most of the stores are still closed. The walkers keep a pretty fast pace because we all have the same objective.

While walking, I love to window shop. One Christmas I picked out everyone's gifts by first window shopping then returning when the stores opened and making a beeline for those specific items. It made my holiday shopping less stressful. I didn't have to fight the wandering crowds. I knew what I wanted and where to get it.

Another thing I do for exercise is clear out the house. I go through every drawer, closet, box, bin, cupboard, shelf, and hiding place, and I gather things to donate or sell. I do this with a lot of energy, so it is a good workout. It makes me feel good because I'm getting exercise, I'm uncluttering my home, I'm getting rid of excess items others could be using, and I'm doing what the Bible instructs:

> *"He that hath two coats,*
> *let him impart to him that hath none..."*
> *Luke 3:11*

Actually, I still have more than two coats, but I'm making progress.

Once I get the house cleared out, then I clean with a lot of energy. Getting the house clean is exhausting work. When people ask me if I have exercise equipment, I say, "Yes, I have a vacuum cleaner, a mop, a broom, scrub brushes, a washer and dryer in the basement, a lawn mower, and hedge trimmer."

Note: Cleaning is not a gender-specific nor age-restricted activity. Everyone living in the home is responsible for keeping the place clean and in order.

Another great way to get out and get moving is to volunteer. Look for something physically taxing where you are on your feet and moving. We volunteered at the Mid-Ohio Food Bank where we sorted and boxed donated food. We shared a few laughs with other volunteers and got a real workout.

Volunteering helps put problems in perspective. There are people who are in desperate need. I forget that sometimes. We have been given much. We can share.

Add or Increase These

What does the Bible say to eat?

"And God said,
Behold, I have given you every herb bearing seed,
which is upon the face of all the earth,
and every tree in which is the fruit of a tree yielding seed;
to you it shall be for meat."
Genesis 1:29-30

"Every moving thing that liveth shall be meat for you;
even as the green herb have I given you all things."
Genesis 9:3

That doesn't sound like it includes some of those items I can't pronounce that are listed on the ingredients labels.

Healthful food is a means to an end. It is fuel for the body. Let the objective of mealtime be to refuel and to have fellowship with family and friends.

Fruits and Vegetables. The recommendation used to be to have at least five servings of fruits and vegetables each day. With all the highly processed fast foods available, junk food options, and busy schedules, many of us have to make a determined effort to consume fresh fruits and vegetables. The latest information from the government tells us to "Make half your plate fruits and vegetables." [xxvi]

Good nutrition is important for good health. From my experience, when I stick to a diet of fresh fruits and vegetables, I feel energetic. I feel good.

It helps to plan ahead. If I don't have healthful foods around when I'm hungry, I'll grab whatever is quick and available. Do you do that too? If there are apples or bananas, I'll grab one of those; but if there are cookies, I'm likely to grab one of those.

At a Weight Watchers® meeting a few years ago one of the members talked about getting "the slammers." When you have "the slammers," you go into the kitchen and open every cupboard door and the refrigerator door looking for something "good." People in the next room hear doors slamming. To avoid "the slammers," have a bowl of fruit on the counter and other healthful treats where anyone can easily find them.

If you think you don't like vegetables, change your mind. You can do that. Start with something you think you might like a little, and then find recipes that make it even more appealing. Try a wider variety of vegetables. Go to a restaurant with a buffet and see what they offer. Have a bite of something you have never tried. You might find something you enjoy.

When my eating habits changed, my taste preferences changed. Our bodies adjust to the taste of the amounts of sugar, salt, and fat we eat until we can no longer taste they may be excessive.[xxvii] I started eating more naturally and foods I used to enjoy began to taste awful. Vegetables and fruits tasted better as I reduced sugar, salt, and fat intake from processed foods.

Vitamins. You can get most of the needed vitamins from a well-balanced diet, but you should talk to your Chiropractor or other healthcare professional trained in nutrition to find out if you need vitamin supplements.

Reduce or Avoid These

What does the Bible say to avoid? There are some instructions in Leviticus Chapter 11 and Deuteronomy Chapter 14. It is beneficial for you to review what is written there and to discuss it with your religious leaders to determine what is right for you.

Sugar and Caffeine. I need to avoid sugar and caffeine. I find sugar and caffeine make my anxiety worse. After the car accident when I was in a severe state of depression, I lived on pop and chocolate and had a lot of fat in my diet until one day I noticed I was upset and often crying about the same time every day. After a lunch that usually included pop, a cheeseburger, and fries, I would get hungry again at about 2:00. I would drag myself to the candy machines and get another pop and candy bar. I would get a quick boost and then crash worse than before. Within 45 minutes, I would be overly upset about something minor. It took me awhile to recognize the pattern of cause and effect. When I was depressed, the impact was much more evident. When I became healthier, sugar did not have such an impact on my physical and mental well-being.

If you plan to reduce your sugar intake, be sure to read ingredients labels. I went through my cupboards and found sugar (and high-fructose corn syrup) in products such as peanut butter, bread, canned fruit, canned vegetables, mayonnaise, and spaghetti sauce. I even found sugar as an ingredient of vegetable soup labeled "healthy." Why would vegetable soup need sugar? My can of vegetarian vegetable soup contained high fructose corn syrup. That just doesn't sound right.

I also avoid artificial sweeteners.

I have a strong reaction to caffeine. Even a small amount will keep me charged up for hours.

A Good Resource. Dr. Don Colbert[xxviii], author of "Eat This and Live," has several books addressing certain conditions like diabetes. He gives advice about good food choices and what to avoid.

Think about it: Yesterday I decided to stop consuming pop and chocolate. Tonight I have an awful headache and some nausea. I am experiencing withdrawal. If sugar, high fructose corn syrup, and caffeine are good for my body, why am I having withdrawal? You don't get this kind of physical reaction if you miss a day without fresh fruits or vegetables. Why such a bad reaction from missing a day without caffeine and sugar?

More Good Health Options

<u>**Water Filter**</u>. A water pitcher with a filter makes water taste better. When it tastes better, I drink more. When I drink more, waste is flushed out more efficiently, and my body stays hydrated. I always have a fresh pitcher of filtered water in the refrigerator. I use filtered water when cooking and in the cat's water dish too.

Water filter pitchers and replacement filters might seem a little expensive, but they are well worth it for your good health. If my pitcher broke, I would replace it immediately.

Air Filter. I have a short-haired cat and I'm amazed how much fur he loses. I use a floor model HEPA air filter and it does a nice job of keeping fur, dust, and stuff out of the air. The air in my home feels fresher when I run the air filter. When I use it in my bedroom, I seem to sleep better.

Natural Products. I believe I am treating my body to a healthier lifestyle by replacing soap, shampoo, toothpaste, deodorant, and cleaning products with natural, organic, environmentally-friendly products when possible and when it makes sense.

Pray about this and take steps to have a healthier home and a healthier body, and feel more energized.

S.L.E.E.P.

"...and thy sleep shall be sweet."
Proverbs 3:24

If you are experiencing stress and anxiety, chances are you are also having trouble getting enough sleep. I'd like to share a little trick to help. I use an acronym to attack the problem from all sides.

I use S.L.E.E.P. as an acronym for:
 S = Same time
 L = Lights out
 E = Eat smart
 E = Ease on down
 P = Postpone worry

Let's look at each of those in more detail.

S = Same Time. Get into a routine. Go to bed at the same time each night and get up at the same time each morning. Set a schedule to allow for eight hours of sleep. Eight hours is commonly recommended. You might need a little more or a little less. If possible, keep the schedule even on days when you could stay up late or sleep in.

Sometimes I struggle with this one because I like to stay up late on weekends. When I keep my schedule even on weekends, I feel better and Monday morning is less stressful because I am rested.

Set your sleeping schedule to fit your lifestyle or situation. It does not matter if you go to bed at 9:00 p.m. or 2:00 a.m. The important elements are (1) consistency and (2) getting eight hours of uninterrupted sleep.

Keep the alarm clock set at the same time every day of the week.

L = Lights Out. Earlier I mentioned how light makes your body react like it is daytime. Turn off the lights or at least turn them down so you can fall asleep more naturally. A dark bedroom will usually cause your body to react like it is night time.

E = Eat Smart. There are certain foods to which I react strongly. Observe what you eat in the hours before bedtime and see if you can make a connection as well.

Some people have trouble with caffeine. I cannot have anything with caffeine after 4:00 p.m. or I will be awake until well after midnight.

Salt is another food that keeps some people awake.

Your reaction to certain foods may be different from mine. Notice what you eat before bedtime and observe your body's reaction.

Foods with a strong flavor or lots of grease will keep me awake. And, if I have something spicy, the taste will linger and prevent me from falling asleep peacefully. On the other hand, a light snack before bedtime will satisfy my hunger, and I will drift off to sleep more easily.

You may have noticed how Thanksgiving turkey puts the family to sleep. A chemical in turkey is relaxing, so turkey is a good evening snack.

E = Ease on Down. If you are rushing around or doing vigorous exercise or chores, and then you lie down to go to sleep, it will take awhile for your body to relax. Allow for relaxing downtime before bed to help you fall asleep more easily.

Reading or taking a warm bath is a good way to relax.

It also helps to have a bedroom that is peaceful and free of clutter. Clutter sends the message that chores are not done, or there is chaos in your life.

P = Postpone Worry. I know this is easier said than done.

The technique I use is to keep a pad and pen by the bed and when needed, I jot down a few notes about what is bothering me. Then, I pray and put the problem in God's hands. At that moment, it is more important to turn my attention to sleep.

Think of loving, peaceful thoughts while falling asleep.

Getting enough rest helps me tackle my problems fresh in the morning.

It has been my experience that if I ask God for help then let go and fall asleep, often answers and options will pop in my mind in the morning.

Try this technique to postpone your worrying until morning.

"I will both lay me down in peace, and sleep:
for thou Lord, only makest me dwell in safety."
Psalm 4:8

Other Sleep Suggestions. Here are more suggestions that might help.

Grandma used to pray us to sleep. When we would spend the night with Grandma and be wiggling all over the place the way little kids do, Grandma would start praying and continue until we fell asleep. I still like to pray myself to sleep.

I have taken an occasional sleeping pill, but I don't like doing it. It makes me sleep but it is not a restful sleep, and it can be difficult to shake off the drowsy feeling the next day.

Increase your level of physical activity during the day so your body gets tired.

"Blessed is the person
who is too busy to worry in the daytime
and too sleepy to worry at night."
Author Unknown

Sleep Deficit Problems. I find when I'm tired, everything seems more difficult, my nerves are jittery, and I am more likely to jump at other people. If I have a good night's sleep, it is easier to manage my mood and stress level.

Did you know sleep deprivation can cause you to gain weight?[xxix] I've seen this in my own life. When I don't get enough sleep, I try to substitute food for sleep. I get drowsy at work and grab something to eat to get an energy boost. When I am tired, my body doesn't need extra calories; it needs sleep.

The Center for Disease Control (CDC) website says, "Insufficient sleep is associated with a number of chronic diseases and conditions – such as diabetes, cardiovascular disease, obesity, and depression – which threaten our nation's health." [xxx]

That's pretty strong.

A teenager physically needs more sleep than an adult to function properly.[xxxi] I know a person who kept waking up her teenager and calling him lazy because he was sleeping later in the day or more than she thought he should. She called him lazy but in reality he was not lazy, he was genuinely tired because she was depriving him of his biological need for sleep. (Also, don't call your kids names.)

I find being rested helps my body handle stress better and respond more quickly. Get the rest your body needs and you may find your energy level and outlook will improve.

Summary of Energize Tools from this Chapter

- Keep God's Words in your heart.

   o *"He that hath two coats, let him impart to him that hath none..." Luke 3:11*

   o *"And God said, Behold, I have given you every herb bearing seed, which is upon the face of all the earth, and every tree in which is the fruit of a tree yielding seed; to you it shall be for meat." Genesis 1:29-30*

   o *"Every moving thing that liveth shall be meat for you; even as the green herb have I given you all things." Genesis 9:3*

   o *"...and thy sleep shall be sweet." Proverbs 3:24*

   o *"I will both lay me down in peace, and sleep: for thou Lord, only makest me dwell in safety." Psalm 4:8*

- Let others inspire you.

  - *"Blessed is the person who is too busy to worry in the daytime and too sleepy to worry at night."* Author Unknown

- The letter "E" in the P.R.A.I.S.<u>E</u>. G.O.D. toolbelt holds the tool "Energize."

- Remember to watch your diet and keep physically active to stay energized when under a lot of stress so your body can handle stress-related chemicals more efficiently.

- Make lifestyle changes to become healthier. Even small changes can have big benefits.

- Realize better health is a choice. You can choose to feel better and take action to make that happen.

- Pray about this and take steps to have a healthier home and a healthier body.

- Consult a Chiropractor or other person trained in nutrition to help guide you in making the right food choices.

- Reduce the amount of sugar in your diet and add more healthful foods.

- If you think you don't like vegetables, change your mind. There are lots of options. Find recipes that make vegetables more appealing to you.

- Plan ahead and have healthful choices available for when you want a snack.

- Read ingredients labels on canned, packaged, or processed foods so you know what you are consuming.

- Observe your body's reaction to things like sugar, salt, and caffeine. Figure out what gives you a negative physical reaction.

- Change your perspective about food. It is fuel. Mealtime is an opportunity for fellowship and bonding with folks we love.

- Use a water filter and an air filter.

- Avoid foods that keep you awake.

- Consult your doctor to see if you have physical limitations to becoming more active.

- Find a sport or activity you enjoy, decide on a schedule, and make a commitment.

- Become involved in an activity or sport to redirect your thoughts to something more beneficial and positive than any stressful things you may be experiencing.

- Find a gym, YMCA, or fitness center if you like, but know there are also cheaper alternatives like walking, running, or even cleaning the house vigorously.

- Treat your body to a healthful lifestyle. Whenever possible and practical, consume natural, organic foods and use natural products.

- Get 8 hours of sleep. Remember to S.L.E.E.P.
  - S = Same time.
  - L = Lights out.
  - E = Eat smart.
  - E = Ease on down.
  - P = Postpone worry

Tool #8

Goals

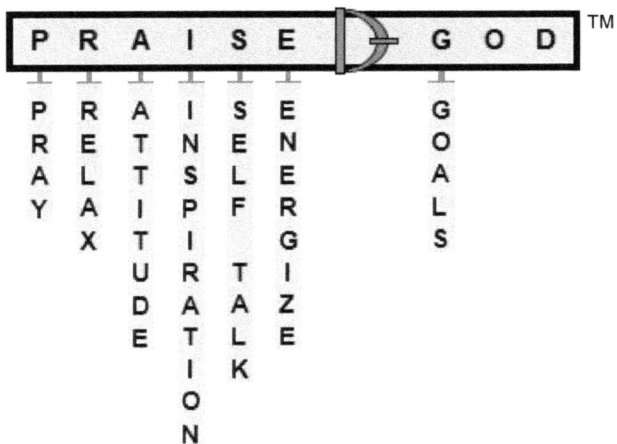

PRAISE GOD™

PRAY RELAX ATTITUDE INSPIRATION SELF TALK ENERGIZE GOALS

The letter "G" in the P.R.A.I.S.E. G.O.D. toolbelt represents Goals. This tool is about how setting and accomplishing goals can:

- Distract us from stressful thoughts and feelings.

- Move us away from difficult situations and toward what we really want.

- Show us proof we can accomplish things.

Since the purpose of this toolbelt is to help reduce anxiety, we are going to focus on setting realistic goals. This exercise is designed to make your life easier, not harder.

The King James Version of the Holy Bible does not use the word "goal." Other interpretations do use it so I'm including those scriptures in the King James Version text.

These passages from Corinthians encourage us to focus on the prize (the goal) and to go for it:

"Knowing ye not that they which run in a race run all,
but one receiveth the prize? So run, that ye may obtain."
1 Corinthians 9:24

Even if you don't see other people competing for the prize or goal you desire, realize time wasting activities and other distractions compete for your attention and can stop you from obtaining what you really want. Keep your eyes on the prize.

Don't just beat the air, have clearly defined goals.

"I therefore so run not as uncertainly;
so fight I, not as one that beateth the air:"
1 Corinthians 9:26

This reminds me of when we do a lot of activity but never actually accomplish anything.

Do you have goals? Most people do not. Setting a goal or goals can make a difference in your life. I've seen it happen in mine.

> *"This one step –*
> *choosing a goal and sticking to it –*
> *changes everything."*
> Scott Reed [xxxii]

While pursuing your goals, you evolve into a more productive, confident person.

> *"What you get by achieving your goals*
> *is not as important as what you become*
> *by achieving your goals."*
> Zig Ziglar[xxxiii]

Many of us have dreams, but we keep them as dreams. Once you change your dream to a goal and take action, you can make your dream come true.

> *"A dream becomes a goal*
> *the moment you write it down.*
> *A goal becomes a plan*
> *the moment you break it down into doable steps.*
> *A plan becomes a reality only when you take action."*
> Marshall Sylver [xxxiv]

Setting goals brings your dreams into focus. You might be thinking for whatever reason, you can't have your dream. Please consider going through this process anyway and see what happens. Your dreams might be closer than you think. Make your dream a goal.

Goals Can Build Your Confidence

When I set a goal and achieve it, I keep evidence to remind myself of my strength, my focus, and my capabilities. During those times when I am down and lose confidence, I look at the evidence of what I have achieved and it gives me strength.

For example, going on vacation without going into debt was a great goal for me. I worked hard to save the money to go, I made arrangements, and then we took a fun trip. This was an achievement because it was not easy since I was raising my child by myself. It shows my commitment as a responsible, loving parent. I keep the photographs not only as a reminder of how much fun we had but also to prove I accomplished things in the past; therefore, I know I can accomplish things in the future. I can set another goal with confidence. I did it once; I can do it again.

Do I sometimes set goals and fail? Yes, but I set more goals and try again. I am controlling this so I can make adjustments as needed and keep going.

This is an opportunity to let setting goals build your confidence. If you want your dreams to come true, make them goals and take action. The time to take a shot at having the life you want is now.

> *"You miss 100% of the shots you never take."*
> Wayne Gretzky [xxxv]

When you know what you want or as my brother says, "Get fire in your belly," nothing can stop you from taking action.

Goals

Let's look at some general information:
- Personal goals
- Dream crushers

- Setting goals

Personal Goals. You might already have family goals, work-related goals, or goals in other areas of your life, but we are going to focus on setting personal goals. In this exercise you will identify and define goals for yourself. The toolbelt is all about you and helping you become stronger and empowered. The goal-setting tool helps you find direction and take control.

Important Note: Your goal can't be to make someone else change. That would need to be their goal, not yours. Identify a goal YOU can do for yourself.

Dream Crushers. You may not recognize them as such, but there are probably dream crushers somewhere in your life so I do not believe you should tell your personal goal to anyone. This is private. You greatly reduce your chance of success by telling someone your goal.

When you tell a friend or loved one your goal and start to change, it may upset or frighten them because they may consciously or subconsciously believe it will change the relationship. They may react negatively. Keep your goal to yourself, continue on your path, and allow relationships to evolve naturally.

There may be some people who will be critical because they are not capable of giving you encouragement and support. This is not a reflection of you but an issue within them.

Some may belittle your goals and tell you all the wonderful things they have done. Their ego gets in the way of them supporting you.

Some dream crushers will start needling you to report your progress. It sounds supportive, but it can be discouraging. They may also keep track and remind you of when you stumble.

Keep your goals to yourself. Don't go through all the work of defining a goal that is in your heart, and then risk having it crushed.

"Keep away from people who try to belittle your ambitions.
Small people always do that,
but the really great make you feel
that you, too, can become great."
Mark Twain

Setting Goals. Set goals that are a stretch, a bit out of your comfort zone, or a challenge, but attainable.

Avoid discussing and comparing your goals to someone else's goals. God made you delightfully unique. You have your own path.

We think in pictures. Set a goal where you can see the result in your mind.

Set a time limit for each goal. It will help you stay on track if you have a deadline.

Avoid letting someone else set a goal for you. Your goals must suit you. Your life is not a game being played by other people. This is a serious matter between you and your Creator. If God is directing you towards something that needs your attention, you don't need anyone else to be in agreement.

Finally, one reason we go to counselors or whine to friends is because we are fired up about something and we need to blow off steam. It works and we feel better afterward. With goals, we get fired up at the possibilities and this creates a lot of energy, which we do *not* want to dissipate. Keep your goals private and use that energy for motivation and action.

Goal Ladders™

Let's find a goal and think of ways to reach that goal. At first, the goal might look like it is too big so we start breaking it down until we have something that can be done easily.

I have developed a set of Goal Ladders™ that use the tools from the P.R.A.I.S.E. G.O.D. toolbelt.

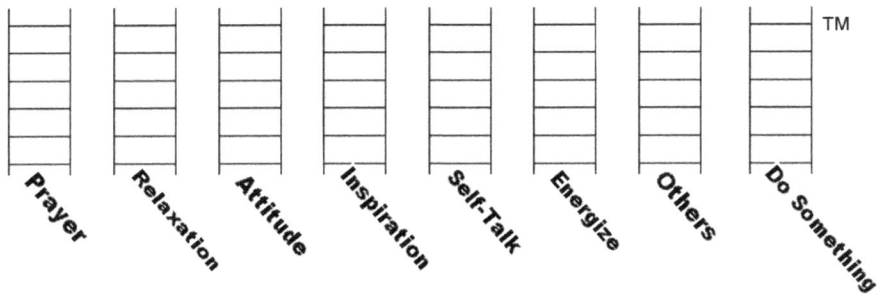

The procedure is to look at the first ladder, labeled here as "Prayer" and shade in the rungs from the bottom up to your level of comfort. The bottom rung means not comfortable. The top rung means very comfortable, not a problem area.

Each person defines the ladder differently. The ladder can be about the amount of time you spend in prayer, knowing what the Holy Bible says about prayer, the number of prayers you have memorized, wanting to learn more about how prayer can improve your life, or something else. It's up to you.

Take a few moments to think about prayer and shade in the rungs from the bottom up. There is no right or wrong decision.

Repeat the process on each ladder. A completed set of ladders might look like this:

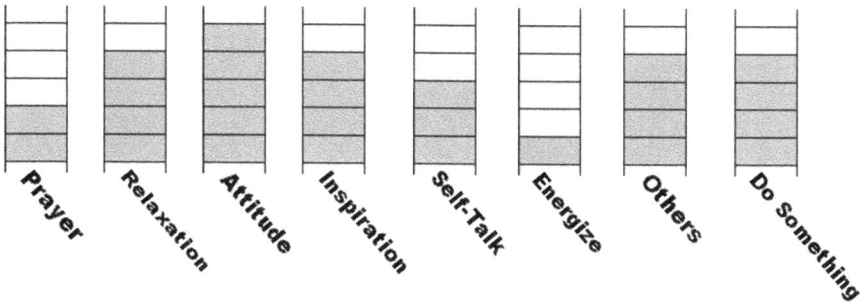

Looking at this example of a completed set of ladders, I feel pretty comfortable except in the area of being Energized. When I got to the Energize ladder, I not only had a logical reason for my choice, I also had a strong negative feeling so I could only shade in one rung. THAT is the ladder we want to address.

Feelings, negative or positive, are motivating. This is an area where there is the greatest chance of success.

What can I do to become more energized? I can do this every day: Walk or workout, enjoy at least two fruits and two vegetables, take a multivitamin, drink six glasses of water, and get eight hours of sleep. That's a lot and I'm already overwhelmed so let's see what it looks like on Goal Ladders™.

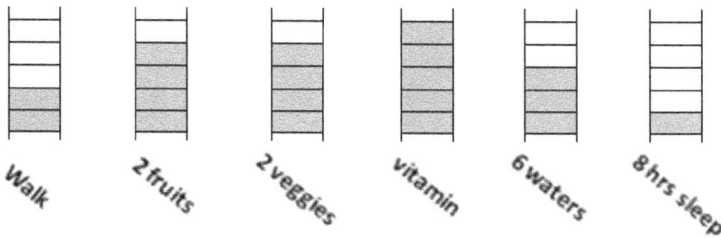

The area where I have the most problem is not getting enough sleep. What can I do to get more sleep? I can do this: (1) Get rid of the clutter that reminds me of all the work I need to do, (2) finish daily chores, and (3) relax before going to bed. That still seems like a lot. Let's see what it looks like on Goal Ladders™.

No clutter   Chores done   Relax before bedtime

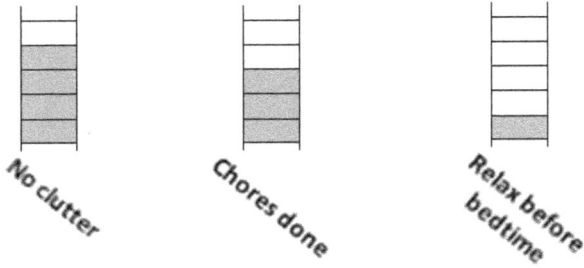

Relaxing before going to bed is revealed as a problem area. When I rush around trying to get everything done before going to bed, I lie in bed and my heart and mind are still racing. What can I do to relax before going to bed? I can do this: (1) Have at least three books at my bedside so I can have a choice of something to read to get my mind off my worries. (2) Have a note by my bedside where I have written the time I will turn off the lights and the time I will set the alarm to wake up so I get a full eight hours of restful sleep. (3) Turn off the TV at 10:00 (or another time you choose), an hour before lights out, to signal my body clock it is night so it will release melatonin and I can fall asleep naturally. Let's put this on Goal Ladders™.

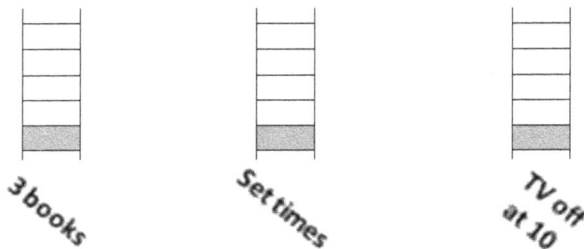

3 books   Set times   TV off at 10

These are three things I don't do now but could do easily. I have broken this down into manageable, clearly defined goals I can start doing immediately. These are goals I can determine without question whether or not they have been accomplished. These simple goals will help me get the sleep I need and improve my energy level.

Example

FIRST LEVEL

Prayer Relaxation Attitude Inspiration Self-Talk Energize Others Do Something

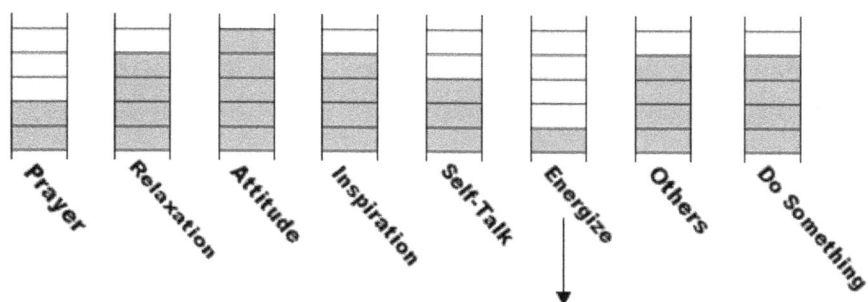

SECOND LEVEL - Energize

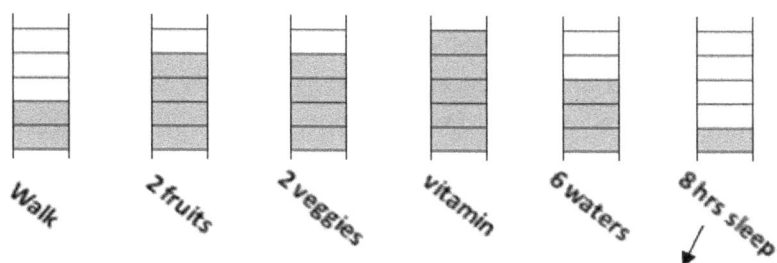

Walk 2 fruits 2 veggies vitamin 6 waters 8 hrs sleep

THIRD LEVEL – Get 8 hours of sleep each night

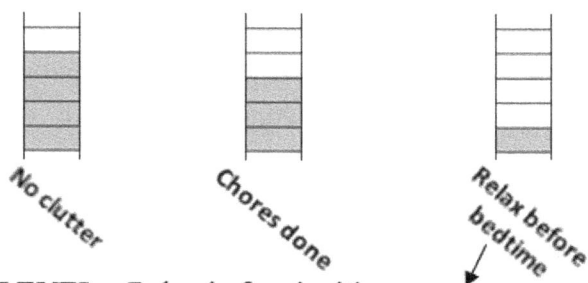

No clutter Chores done Relax before bedtime

FOURTH LEVEL – Relax before bedtime

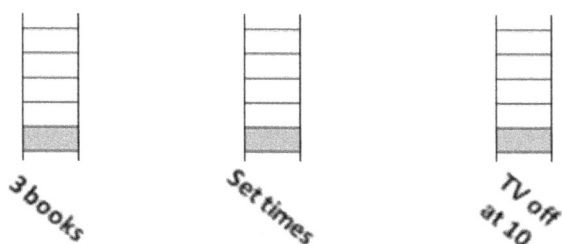

3 books Set times TV off at 10

There is no limit to the number of levels. What is important is you are able to identify clear goals.

You can work on more than one goal at a time, but working on everything at once can set yourself up to be overwhelmed and discouraged. Make this easy, fun, and manageable. Enjoy each success.

Each goal you accomplish and each problem you conquer should make your life easier.

When one area is under control, go back to the beginning, start with a new set of ladders, and do the exercise again. Start at the beginning again because this tool changes as you grow and change. When goals are accomplished, previously shaded ladders may no longer be relevant. Do the process again starting from the beginning to identify the next area on which to focus.

Set a Goal

This is a written exercise. There is something powerful about writing down your goals. It solidifies dreams and random thought into a specific direction or plan.

You might glance at all the ladders and think, "I'll do this one." But, that isn't as useful as prayerfully taking time to examine each one. While doing this, an unexpected thought or insight might lead you in a surprising new direction.

There will be areas you don't want to face, and that's fine. But, there will be areas you are drawn to and want to explore.

This activity is best done alone. Asking others for input is not useful because they cannot feel what you are feeling, and they might not understand all the dynamics that go into your choices.

Prayerfully ask God to guide you to identify a goal.

The only meaning a ladder has is the meaning you give it.

1. <u>First Level</u>. Identify a goal area. (Shade in the rungs.)

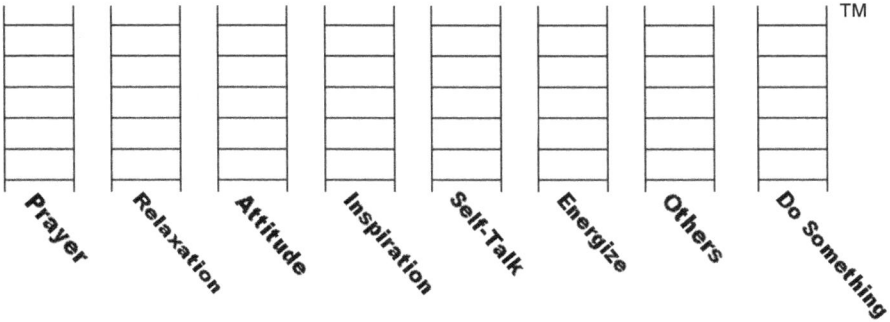

2. Choose the ladder you want to work on: _____
    Example: *Energize*.

3. <u>Second Level</u>. What could be done to improve that area? Put those ideas under Goal Ladders^{TM} and shade in the rungs up to your comfort lever. Use as many or few ladders as needed.

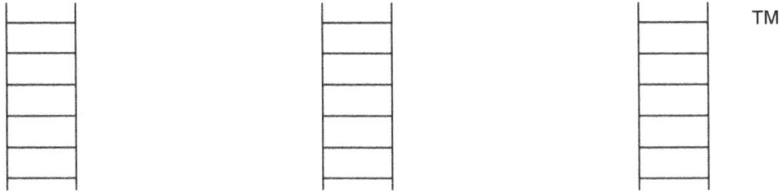

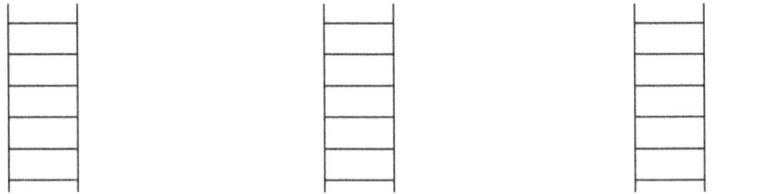

4. Choose a ladder you want to work on.

5. <u>Third Level</u>. What could be done to improve that area? Put those ideas under another set of Goal Ladders^{TM} and shade in the rungs up to your comfort lever. Use as many or as few ladders as needed.

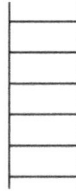

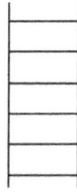

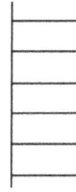

Have you been able to identify one or more clear, attainable goal(s)? If not, identify a ladder you wish to break down further and create another set of Goal Ladders^{TM}.

6. <u>Fourth Level</u>. Look at the previous set of Goal Ladders^{TM} and identify where you would like to focus. What could be done to improve that area? Put those ideas under another set of Goal Ladders^{TM} and shade in the rungs up to your comfort level.

If needed, there is a blank set of Goal Ladders^{TM} in Appendix A you can copy for your own use.

 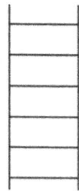 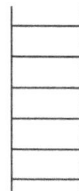

TM

 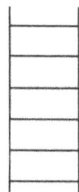 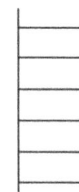

If you want to keep track of your accomplishments, use a Goal Success Record.

Goal Success Record
Goal: _____
_____
_____
Date Accomplished: _____

I REACHED MY GOAL!

"The rung of a ladder was never meant to rest upon,
but only to hold a man's foot long enough
to enable him to put the other somewhat higher."
Thomas Henry Huxley [xxxvi]

At one of the lowest points of my life, I had a goal of just getting through another day. My Goal Ladders™ were pretty sad. It took most of my energy to get to work on time and hang in there for eight hours. When I got home, I didn't do anything until the next day. I didn't have much of a life, but little by little I was able to make minor changes, achieve goals, and climb out of my despair. They were small steps, but I just kept going in the right direction.

"If we are facing in the right direction,
all we have to do is keep on walking."
Buddhist Proverb

You may be at a similar point. Be good to yourself. Use this exercise to identify something you can do to make your situation better and to make you feel better. It doesn't have to be something huge, just something better. Even small accomplishments can help you feel stronger and more in control of your life.

A Final Word about Goals. I have a dear friend who became fascinated with finding out about her ancestry. As she became more involved, she learned where different ones were buried. She visited gravesites to take photographs of the inscriptions.[xxxvii] While there, she told me she noticed many old stones were hard to read because the inscriptions had worn off. The stone was there, but the information was gone.

This started me thinking about what we leave behind. Just like us, these people lived, loved, worked, laughed, and dreamed. They died and in time were forgotten except for a stone in the cemetery. What were their dreams and goals? Life is so short.

Why not set a goal that will enrich your life and the lives of those you love? Why not make a goal that will benefit others long after you and I are gone? Perhaps now that you are finding ways to get beyond the anxiety and fear that has held you back, you have an amazing adventure waiting for you and an opportunity to achieve incredible goals. Why not go big and live your life to the fullest?

Summary of Goal Tools from this Chapter

- Keep God's Words in your heart.

  - *"Knowing ye not that they which run in a race run all, but one receiveth the prize? So run, that ye may obtain."* 1 Corinthians 9:24

  - *"I therefore so run not as uncertainly; so fight I, not as one that beateth the air"* 1 Corinthians 9:26

- Let others inspire you.

  - *"This one step – choosing a goal and sticking to it – changes everything."* Scott Reed

  - *"What you get by achieving your goals is not as important as what you become by achieving your goals."* Zig Ziglar

  - *"A dream becomes a goal the moment you write it down. A goal becomes a plan the moment you break it down into doable steps. A plan becomes a reality only when you take action."* Marshall Sylver

  - *"You miss 100% of the shots you never take."* Wayne Gretzky

  - *"The rung of a ladder was never meant to rest upon, but only to hold a man's foot long enough to enable him to put the other somewhat higher."* Thomas Henry Huxley o *"If we are facing in the right direction, all we have to do is keep on walking."* Buddhist Proverb

- The letter "G" in the P.R.A.I.S.E. <u>G</u>.O.D. toolbelt holds the tool "Goals."

- The purpose of setting goals is to empower you and build your confidence so you can more easily manage the challenges of anxiety.

- Goal setting can be a fun and enlightening experience. Use goal setting to make your life more enjoyable.

- Use goals to help you move forward with your life when you feel stuck.

- Turn your dream into a goal. Write it down, make it clear, and start to work on the steps needed to reach your goal.

- You can't hit a target you can't see. Define a goal to bring the target into focus.

- The goal-setting exercise is most useful if you do it thoughtfully and prayerfully.

- Keep your goals private. God made you delightfully unique so what is right for you might not be right for someone else. If you share your goal with someone, they could discourage you because of their perspective.

- Setting and achieving goals empowers you. Having someone else set your goals or monitor your progress keeps you weak.

- Remember to set goals only for yourself. You cannot set a goal for someone else to do something or to change. Release the stress of thinking you are responsible to change someone else.

- Set clearly defined goals. A clearly defined goal can help you identify what you want, move you in a positive direction, inspire you to achieve, build your confidence, let you feel the joy of accomplishment, and profoundly change the direction of your life.

- Use the Goal Ladders™ to identify an area you would like to improve.

- Use the Goal Ladders™ to chunk down or drill down until you are able to define manageable goals, steps, or tasks. There is no set number of ladders. Use what you need. Use as many levels as you need.

- Use logic *and* emotion to help you define your Goal Ladders™ and your goals. Emotions, negative or positive, are motivating. Focus on what you are emotionally drawn to and what will motivate you.

- Complete *all* the Goal Ladders™ thoughtfully and prayerfully and something unexpected may be revealed.

- Set goals that are a stretch but attainable. Give yourself a challenge and your sense of accomplishment will be greater.

- This is a written exercise. Don't try to bypass this step. There is something powerful about writing down your goals. It solidifies dreams and random thoughts into a specific plan of action.

- Write down your goals and put them where you will see them often.

- Keep a journal, photos, mementos, or some other physical reminder of goals you have accomplished so you have visual proof that you can improve your situation.

- If you set a goal and are not able to accomplish it, set another one and keep going.

- Not all problems are simple, so not all goals can be simplified. If you are facing a huge problem, look for anything you can do to make it better, no matter how small.

- Take time to enjoy your feeling of success for each goal you complete. Use that feeling of accomplishment to inspire and motivate yourself to move to the next goal.

- When your problems seem overwhelming and you don't feel you can do much, a little is okay. Just start going in the direction you want to go even if it is very slow progress at first.

- Thank God for His help and guidance.

Tool #9
Others

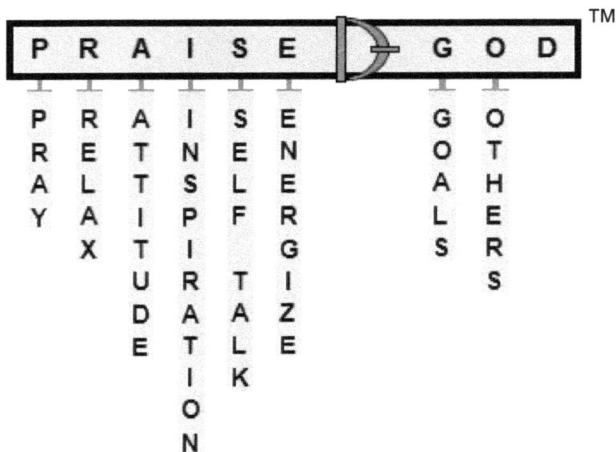

PRAISE GOD™

P	R	A	I	S	E	G	O	D
PRAY	RELAX	ATTITUDE	INSPIRATION	SELF TALK	ENERGIZE	GOALS	OTHERS	

The letter "O" in our acronym P.R.A.I.S.E. G.O.D. represents *Others*. There are two tools for this letter.

- *In Service to Others*.
- *In Association with Others*.

In Service to Others

> *"Inasmuch as ye have done it*
> *unto one of the least of these my brethren,*
> *ye have done it unto me."*
> Matthew 25:40

They Need You. Robert Sargent Shriver was instrumental in the creation of the Peace Corps and Job Corps. These are his words about service to others:

> *"Break that mirror in front of you,*
> *that mirror that only lets you look at yourself.*
> *Break it so that you can look beyond.*
> *You'll see the rest of the world.*
> *You'll see people who need your help."*
> Sargent Shriver [xxxviii]

What powerful words. There are other people who desperately need your help and your prayers. When we are anxious, depressed, or worried, we are looking at ourselves and our own situations, which is natural and expected. But if we can look outside ourselves, our problems can diminish as our focus changes.

Your Contribution. Don't underestimate your ability to make a difference in the life of someone else. Small effort on your part might make a world of difference to a person in need. I remember a time in my life when I was feeling alone and isolated. A man walked by and simply said, "Hello." He smiled warmly before he hurried on his way. It's funny, but it made me feel connected again. Such a small thing made a difference to my state of mind.

You might be shaking your head thinking the world is a mess and wondering if you can make a difference. You *can* make a difference. All you need is the willingness to help and a prayer that God will lead you where He wants.

> *"The deeds you do may be the only sermon*
> *some persons will hear today."*
> Saint Francis of Assisi

I saw a YouTube video of a man explaining that he and his wife get sturdy bags and fill them with some basic items and then give the bags to homeless people. I thought that was a great idea, so I got a couple of my extra bags and asked my friend if she had any extra bags or totes to donate. Together we filled ten bags with items like peanut butter, crackers, washcloth, soap, razor, gloves, candy, note pad, pen, tissue, deodorant, and socks, and then delivered them to the soup kitchen to be given to anyone in need. It didn't take any special skill to do this. (We've donated 60 bags so far!)

The needs of homeless people are easy to see, but also remember everyone is dealing with something. Everyone. You can't tell by looking at someone what it is or what it's doing to their life. Outward appearance doesn't necessarily show inward turmoil. Someone who appears to be at peace may actually be very much in need of your warm smile and compassion.

"Be kind,
for everyone you meet
is fighting a hard battle."
Plato[xxxix]

What You Have to Give. Each of us can do something to make the world better.

"As every man hath received the gift,
even so minister the same one to another,
as good stewards of the manifold grace of God."
1 Peter 4:10

We have been given different talents and we would do well to use them for the glory of God. (Matthew 25:15-30)

Be open to a wide variety of possibilities of what you can do.

I know a lady whose life mission seems to be helping dogs and rescuing a certain breed of dog. Randi is passionate about her work. I often get emails from her about a lost pet, an animal that needs money for a medical procedure, or activities for her favorite organization, *Stop the Suffering*[xl]. She works tirelessly for her furry friends. Her passion shows through her actions, and she is doing wonderful work. She is making the world around her better. She is very proactively helping as many of God's creatures as she can.

When I was a child, we had the most wonderful neighbor, Alice Williamson. If she heard any of us children were ill, she would rush over with a glass of 7Up in a special cup with a lacy doily (fancy napkin) on top and perhaps a sprig of mint or a tiny flower from her garden. It made the sick child feel loved.

You can do something to brighten someone else's day. Let others know you are willing to share what you have learned.

- Are you an excellent cook? Share your cooking tips with the rest of us. Our families will be delighted.

- Do you know how to write an effective resume? Someone you know might not be able to live up to his or her potential unless you share what you know and help them craft an effective resume.

- Do you know something about auto mechanics? Help someone fix a car so he or she can get to his or her job.

- Have you raised a child? A young parent might be struggling and could use your support. Sometimes just letting him or her know you understand their struggle is a very compassionate thing to do.

- Have you figured out a way to overcome an adversity? Tell your story and inspire others.

- Have you picked up some valuable housekeeping tips over the years? You can share your wisdom in a blog or booklet.

- If you are comfortable chatting in smaller groups, decide on a topic you have studied and let others know you would like to share information. For example, start a small discussion group or Bible study. Create a positive environment where you and others can enjoy fellowship and exchange useful ideas.

- Think of something you enjoy and consider teaching it or sharing with others. I'll never forget the kind ladies at the Senior Center who taught a group of fourth-grade children how to knit. Thank you Mrs. McNeal (1900-1989).

- Do you feel your spiritual needs are not being met? Do you see a gap in what is being taught in church? Stop complaining, put together your own Bible-based ministry, start preaching, and become an inspiration for others. Fear of public speaking? Write a book. Publishers don't like your book? Self-publish and sell it on the internet. Can't write? Download "Audacity," a free recording tool, and preach your heart out. Don't think you can do it?

"I can do all things through Christ
which strengtheneth me."
Philippians 4:13

No excuses. Use your talents (Matthew 25:13-30).

Do something to make the world a better place.

"I've learned that you shouldn't go through life
with a catcher's mitt on both hands;
you need to be able to throw something back."
Maya Angelou [xli]

My Mom is a shining example of a life of service. In addition to being a devoted wife, mother, grandmother, great-grandmother, and homemaker for her family, she was very active in our little church and organized groups for other women. She doesn't do any kind of public speaking; she does her work in the background. She works tirelessly behind the scenes to take care of endless details to ensure others have an enjoyable experience.

For several years, Mom volunteered to raise money for the local park. She organized the yearly event, arranged for entertainers and vendors, and secured help from many people in the community. She would put on a festival that energized and blessed the village and at the same time raised thousands of dollars to improve the park, to purchase new playground equipment, and to stock the beautiful lake.

Mom has been a Red Cross Volunteer for more than 30 years. Today at 89, she still volunteers at the hospital one day a week, and she volunteers at a donation center. I think she is amazing. She's always delighted to go to work, and she takes it very seriously. She loves her volunteer work. I'm sure not every moment has been wonderful, but she is dedicated and she is faithful. She is driven by her purpose in life: to serve others.

Mom is also a poet and has written three books, one of treasured family memories, one about her ancestry, and one of her beautiful poetry. Her tremendous attitude of service can be seen in her poem about "Red Cross Volunteers."

RED CROSS VOLUNTEERS

We are the Red Cross volunteers
In pinstriped smocks of blue.
We give our time and energy
To make life nice for you.

We work throughout the hospital,
And greet you at the door.
We give passes and directions
To each and every floor.

The flowers and host of get-well cards
Upon a special cart,
Delivered daily door-to-door
To cheer a patient's heart.

In Unit Lounge, we answer phones
And fill the coffee pots
Liaison for the families
Of those on surgery cots.

The Red Cross staffs the bloodmobile
Teach special classes too
Contact Armed Forces 'round the world
With messages from you.

Sometimes a great disaster strikes
That causes much despair
The clothes, the food, the shelter too
Means Red Cross workers there.

We do not ask for equal pay,
To make our lives worthwhile.
We love to help our fellow man.
Just thank us with a smile.

© 2006 Ruth Moloney Cowgill

What it Does for You. An important benefit of helping others is that it changes your focus. It gives your mind a break from your problems. It changes the direction of your thoughts to a more positive pattern of seeking how you can make someone else's life better.

Focus on your anxiety and it grows. Focus on doing something for someone else and your anxiety diminishes, and another person's life is improved.

Anxiety and stress are often associated with low self-esteem. Being of service to someone in need or volunteering for a worthy cause can make you feel better about yourself because you are making a much needed contribution.

Another aspect of being of service to others is that it brings more good into your life. I believe it is against the laws of nature for prosperity and love to only go one direction. There is a flow that goes through each of us, and when we don't give back, we stop the flow. If we give to others and have a spirit of service, good things flow back into our lives.

"Give, and it shall be given unto you…"
Luke 6:38

This includes tithing. We give because we are asked to do so and because it is important to support our place of worship. But, have you thought of this reason to give: It is beneficial to the giver. Everything already belongs to God. God gives to us all the time. He doesn't need our money. I believe our gifts and tithing show Him our love. We are giving something we value. It shows our dedication to Him. Give because you love Him.

Giving out of love, draws you closer to God.

"Every man according as he purposeth in his heart,
so let him give; not grudgingly, or of necessity:

for God loveth a cheerful giver."
2 Corinthians 9:7

If this subject makes you uncomfortable or if you are hesitant to volunteer, be of service, or give to others, you can start small. When you have more confidence, you can do more. You might find something to do to be of service that will bring great joy into your life.

Take Action. Is there a project, purpose, calling, mission, job, or service on your heart you would like to do that would bless your life and the lives of others? From time to time you might think about something you could do that would be fulfilling to you and would benefit others but you haven't taken action *until now*. Those ideas might be coming from God. He might be telling you what He wants you to do.

In the past, distress, fear, anxiety, sadness, and worry may have discouraged you and held you back, but now you have tools to cope. Go ahead and pray about this and keep your eyes open for opportunities. You don't need to search for what God wants you to do. You only need to pay attention. He will show you.

COMPASSIONATE PEOPLE

Compassionate people,
Warm hearted and true,
Who enrich lives of others
With nice things they do.

Compassionate people,
So precious but few,
Who know in a crisis
The right thing to do.

Compassionate people
Who find joy in giving
And put others first
In their process of living.

When I count my life's blessings
From beginning to end,
I thank God for you,
My Compassionate friend.

© 2006 Ruth Moloney Cowgill

When I was at the lowest place in my life, I could not see any kind of purpose for myself. You might be feeling that way, that you don't have a purpose, and you just want to get through another day. Here is something each of us can do that is one of the most important purposes we have on earth: Pray and praise God with your whole heart. This is so important that if we don't do it, even the stones would cry out. (See Luke 19:40.)

"To our God and Father,
glory forever and ever. Amen"
Philippians 4:20

In Association with Others

Our friends make our days easier because they enrich our lives in so many ways. We are companions for adventures. We share secrets, sorrows, fears, laughter, and fun. A good friend is truly a blessing. I have been blessed with amazing friends, and I thank God for each one of them.

"Two are better than one;
because they have a good reward for their labour.
For if they fail, the one will lift up his fellow;
but woe to him that is alone when he falleth;

for he hath not another to help him up."
Ecclesiastes 4:9-10

Friends are strong because of their combined strengths, and because they can encourage and inspire one another.

Let your friends know how important they are to you.

Relationships Change our Perspective. We form a bond with the people who surround us so it is important to make sure we have healthy relationships.

A relationship that causes you to feel stress, shame, fear, or anxiety is not healthy. In a healthy relationship, each person is supportive of the other. Neither one belittles or tries to control the other. They know a joke at someone else's expense is not a joke, it is abuse. In a healthy relationship, each person likes the other for who they are and they are happy when either one succeeds.

The way I decide if a relationship is healthy is to see how I feel about myself when I am with them. In an unhealthy relationship, I get the message I'm not good enough. In a healthy relationship, I feel good about myself and want to be better. The message might sound similar but notice the subtle difference. One is negative: I'm not good enough. One is positive: I feel good about myself, and this supportive relationship inspires me to grow.

"No person is your friend
who demands your silence,
or denies you the right to grow."
Alice Walker [xlii]

Please understand this is not me judging another person. I'm not labeling a person as unhealthy because I feel bad or uncomfortable when I am with them. I'm evaluating the relationship and saying this relationship is not a good one for me.

Stay in contact with supportive friends and family when you are stressed, and avoid becoming isolated. On occasion when I am depressed, I want to withdraw and be by myself. This is reasonable for a time but after awhile, it is best to be with others. Talk to family and friends. It is not necessary to pour out your problems to them. Just being around someone who cares can divert your attention away from your bad feelings and help you relax.

I've noticed sometimes God sends comforting messages through other people. They might not even know I am struggling, but they say just the thing I need to hear.

Consider reaching out to someone just to chat about things not related to what is bothering you. It makes their day more enjoyable as well as yours.

Facebook can be a great tool for staying connected. I am often awake in the middle of the night. (It is 3:00 a.m. right now.) I like to open Facebook and see who else is awake. I just checked. Ha! Two of my friends are online right now. Hang on, I need to say hello. BRB (be right back).

Remember to be a Friend. It is our privilege to be able to help and support one another. I have wonderful friends and family, and I would do anything for them without question. I want to compassionately support them. Everyone needs support at times. Everyone faces obstacles and challenges, and we are here to help each other. Don't forget to be supportive of your friends.

Energy Drains (Unhealthy Associations). There may be people in your life who need more help than you can provide.

Regardless of how much you care about them, it is not enough. They need professional assistance.

There may be a child, parent, spouse, or friend whose behavior is causing you an extreme amount of anxiety and his or her problems are beyond your ability to solve. You are not responsible for someone else's behavior. You cannot make them strong and healthy. Each person must do his or her work for himself or herself.

It is not in your best interest to have someone drain you emotionally and/or financially. It is not in their best interest to use your support to stay in their unhealthy state. If you do the best you can and it is not enough, refer them to a mental healthcare professional. The right counselor can be an answer to prayer.

"Where no counsel is, the people fall;
but in the multitude of counselors there is safety."
Proverbs 11:14

Your friend or family member may be angry or insulted or try to make you feel guilty about referring them to a professional counselor or to authorities but the bottom line is, if you love them, you want them to have the best possible help, and that help might not be you. Furthermore, you may need to set a firm boundary with them until they get appropriate help.

When you hand over someone to a professional, more than likely, his or her life will improve, and your anxiety will decrease. In addition, a counselor can provide valuable insight to you about how to make boundaries to protect your own health, well-being, and security.

You can't always see the way out when you are inside a very difficult problem or an unhealthy relationship. Your stress level may be an indication you need help from an outside party. Sometimes someone else must point the way.

There are too many people who are in misery, and yet they think they don't need to talk to a trained counselor who could help them.

> *"The way of a fool is right in his own eyes:*
> *but he that hearkeneth unto counsel is wise."*
> *Proverbs 12:15*

Other kinds of energy drains include people who are always gloomy and people who always have some kind of drama going on. They don't have huge problems, and they don't really want your help. For every piece of advice you offer, they have a reason why it won't work. They are oddly comfortable in their self-imposed misery. Often they are very nice people but they have a pitiful outlook on life. I don't think you need to create a boundary with them, just limit your exposure so it doesn't negatively influence *your* outlook. Life is too short to spend time being gloomy or in a constant state of drama.

Don't be an Energy Drain. It is best to avoid making a habit of unloading problems on friends and family. Using them for this purpose can be too much of a burden for them. This is not what you want. I had a problem that went beyond what friends and family could resolve. I was able to find a support group and attend meetings to get valuable, insightful information addressing the specific situation.

New Acquaintances. You may be in a situation where you can expand your circle of friends. When I am in that situation and I meet someone new I use the test I mentioned earlier to see how the new acquaintance makes me feel.

Ask a new acquaintance about his or her interests. They might have a fresh perspective that inspires you to think in a different way. Perhaps you have personalities that just click and you can laugh easily together. They might have interests you've never thought about that sound like a lot of fun. You might have common interests to share.

Your Lead Story. When you are meeting new people, it is worth considering your own lead story. Sometimes meeting new people can make you feel anxious. This will help.

Your lead story is what you use to make that very important first impression. Of course, you think about your hair style and wearing attractive clothing, but what do you say when you first meet someone? What is their first impression of who you are inside? Some people tell really off-the-wall stories when they meet someone.

I met two different women at two different occasions. Within the first 15 minutes here is what they told me:

> Person #1: "My husband drives me crazy, and I had to leave him for awhile so he would straighten up."

> Person #2: "My ex-husband ran off with another woman, so I sold my house and took a trip around the world. It was amazing." (This was several years before the movie "Eat, Pray, Love.")

Person #2 certainly sounds more fun and interesting than the other. What I am illustrating is that their lead stories were quite revealing about who they are and how they approach life.

When you meet someone new, listen to their lead story. They will tell you who they are.

Create your lead story using something positive or something you are excited about. For example, at one time my lead story included that I was working on a Rhubarb Cookbook. I got into the habit of asking people if they had any rhubarb recipes. I got a few but mostly it started a discussion about cooking, family recipes, and so forth. It was a nice conversation starter. And who knows, maybe one day I'll finish that book.

A good way to meet new people is to get involved with something you enjoy. For example, if you have school age children, work with the teacher or Room Parent to help plan holiday parties. You will meet other parents. Talking about your children is a good starting point.

Friends can enrich your life. New friends can add new dimensions and interests to your circle of friends. I remember a rhyme from my childhood about friends that went something like this:

"Make new friends, but keep the old.
One is silver and the other is gold." [xliii]

Summary of Tools from this Chapter

- Keep God's Words in your heart.

    o *"Inasmuch as ye have done it unto one of the least of these my brethren, ye have done it unto me."* *Matthew 25:40*

    o *"As every man hath received the gift, even so minister the same one to another, as good stewards of the manifold grace of God." 1 Peter 4:10*

    o *"I can do all things through Christ which strengtheneth me." Philippians 4:13*

    o *"Give, and it shall be given unto you..." Luke 6:38*

    o *"Every man according as he purposeth in his heart, so let him give; not grudgingly, or of necessity: for God loveth a cheerful giver." 2 Corinthians 9:7*

    o *"To our God and Father, glory forever and ever. Amen" Philippians 4:20* o *"Two are better than one; because they have a good reward for their labour. For if they fail, the one will lift up his fellow; but woe to him that is alone when he falleth; for he hath not another to help him up."* Ecclesiastes 4:9-10

o *"Where no counsel is, the people fall; but in the multitude of counselors there is safety."* Proverbs 11:14

o *"The way of a fool is right in his own eyes: but he that hearkeneth unto counsel is wise."* Proverbs 12:15

o *"My little children, let us not love in word, neither in tongue; but in deed and in truth."* 1 John 3:18

- Let others inspire you.

  o *"Break that mirror in front of you, that mirror that only lets you look at yourself. Break it so that you can look beyond. You'll see the rest of the world. You'll see people who need your help."* Sargent Shriver

  o *"The deeds you do may be the only sermon some persons will hear today."* Saint Francis of Assisi

  o *"Be kind, for everyone you meet is fighting a hard battle."* Plato

  o *"I've learned that you shouldn't go through life with a catcher's mitt on both hands; you need to be able to throw something back."* Maya Angelou

  o *"No person is your friend who demands your silence, or denies you the right to grow."* Alice Walker

  o *"Make new friends, but keep the old. One is silver and the other is gold."*

  o *"Not all of us can do great things. But we can do small things with great love."* Mother Teresa

Tool #9 Others

- The "O" in the P.R.A.I.S.E. G.<u>O</u>.D. toolbelt represents the tool "Others." There are two tools here: In service to others and in association with others.

- Be of service to others. Volunteer, join a service group, or find something you can do for someone. It is healing to look outside ourselves and see what we can do for others. Even small effort on your part might make a world of difference to a person who is hurting or in need.

- Don't underestimate your value and what you can do for others.

- Look for different ways to be of service. Be open to a wide variety of possibilities. Don't dismiss an opportunity without first exploring if it might be something that could be fun for you and helpful to others.

- Look at what touches your heart and become a passionate volunteer.

- Do something to brighten someone else's day.

- Think of a skill you have learned and pass it on to an individual or a group. You know more and have more to give than you might think.

- Have you figured out a way to overcome an adversity? Tell your story and inspire others.

- Being willing to be of service is half the battle. An opportunity will appear.

- Give to help others and let your work be for the glory of God. Count on your reward being in heaven; people won't always thank you.

- Don't judge whether or not the recipient of your good works is worthy. That is not for you to decide. Just continue to do good works.

- Helping someone else gets your mind off your own problems.

- Anxiety, stress, fear, and worry are often associated with low self-esteem. Being of service to someone less fortunate or volunteering for a worthy cause can make you feel better about yourself because you are making a much-needed contribution.

- Give tithes and offerings to demonstrate to God that you love Him.

- There are many opportunities to work with groups or organizations that need you. Find something that is appropriate for you.

- You might feel a need to do something on your own. Do you see a gap in your spiritual needs? Put together your own Bible-based ministry to address that gap and be an inspiration to others. You will learn while you teach.

- Are you anxious about volunteering? Use the tools to help you start small and see where it grows.

- If a service or beneficial project has been on your heart and mind, you now have the tools you need to break through the anxiety and fear. Take action now.

- Associate with people who are positive and supportive.

- A good friend is truly a blessing. Let your friends know how important they are to you.

- We form a bond with people who surround us so it is important to make sure we have healthy relationships.

- In a healthy relationship, you feel good about yourself, and you have support to explore your potential.

- When you are anxious or disheartened, avoid becoming isolated for too long. Stay in contact with people who love you. You don't need to share what is bothering you. Just socialize and it will make you feel better.

- Listen. Sometimes God sends comforting messages through other people. They might not know you are struggling, but they say just the thing you need to hear.

- Remember to be a friend when someone needs you.

- Limit your time with people who are always negative or gloomy or have drama going on. They can drain your energy.

- If there is someone in your life causing you anxiety and draining you emotionally and financially, their problems may be beyond your ability to resolve. Refer them to a professional counselor.

- Set a firm boundary against someone who mistreats you.

- You can't always see the way out when you are inside a very difficult problem or an unhealthy relationship. Someone else must point the way. Don't be afraid to seek counseling for yourself. Don't be afraid to find a different counselor if the first one cannot address your needs.

- Be positive and find positive friends and associates.

- Avoid making a habit of being an energy drain on others.

- Be open to meeting new, positive friends who will enrich your life.

- Seek out friends who believe like you believe.

- Create a great lead story about yourself to use when meeting new people.

Tool #10
Do Something

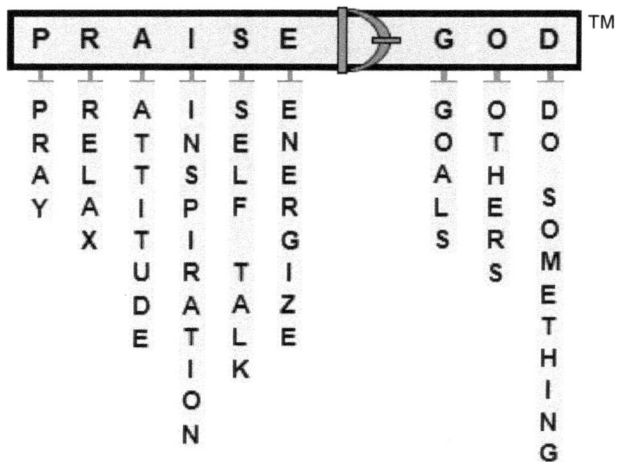

PRAISE GOD™

PRAY
RELAX
ATTITUDE
INSPIRATION
SELF TALK
ENERGIZE

GOALS
OTHERS
DO SOMETHING

In our P.R.A.I.S.E. G.O.D. toolbelt, "D" encourages us to *Do Something*. Take an action step.

> *"Whatsoever thy hand findeth to do,*
> *do it with thy might..."*
> *Ecclesiastes 9:10*

We have all been through stressful, difficult things. There have been many times I felt completely alone. I wanted to give up. At times, life can hurt so much – so many tears. You may have experienced the same. I found if I did nothing, my lack of action prolonged and often intensified the pain. If I took some kind of action, I got through the distress more quickly. I used the tools presented in the toolbelt, and I still use them today.

> *"Regardless of the problem,*
> *the solution is the same:*
> *TAKE ACTION!"*
> Author unknown

Jesus never promised us it would be easy. Our heroes in the Bible did not have easy journeys. We are promised help and blessings along the way and at the end of this life, we will meet the Master, and then we will understand why we had these struggles.

We've just examined a lot of tools, arranged in an easy-to-remember way that can help you do something different from the way you have been doing things. If you do what you did, you'll get what you got -- an overload of anxiety.

> *"If you do what you did,*
> *you'll get what you got."*

From now on, the familiar phrase "PRAISE GOD" has a deeper meaning for you. This phrase needs to be your first and immediate response to everything that happens.

- You are struggling – PRAISE GOD.
- You are hurting – PRAISE GOD.
- You are lonely and afraid – PRAISE GOD.
- The doctor gives you bad news – PRAISE GOD.
- You have to give a presentation – PRAISE GOD.
- You are in a car wreck – PRAISE GOD.
- You are overwhelmed – PRAISE GOD.

When you experience difficult emotions, remember to say, "Praise God." That gets you in touch with the Source of all that is good and opens the toolbelt to your resources.

Bad things happen and it can take time for you to adjust. Eventually we have to go on. These tools can help.

This is an opportunity to take actions to arm yourself with tools to help you and to bring you to a closer walk with God. Use the tools to get beyond the torment in your head and you may find there is an amazing life waiting for you.

Summary of Tools from this Chapter

- Keep God's Words in your heart.

  - *"Whatsoever thy hand findeth to do, do it with thy might..." Ecclesiastes 9:10*

- Let others inspire you.

  - *"Regardless of the problem, the solution is the same: TAKE ACTION!"* Author unknown

  - *"If you do what you did, you'll get what you got."*

  - *"Feel the fear and do it anyway.®"* Susan Jeffers[xliv]

o *"Inaction breeds doubt and fear. Action breeds confidence and courage. If you want to conquer fear, do not sit home and think about it. Go out and get busy."* Dale Carnegie

o *"Don't wait. The time will never be right."* Napoleon Hill

o *"The best way to predict your future is to create it."* Abraham Lincoln

- P.R.A.I.S.E. G.O.<u>D</u>. = Do Something.

- Do things differently than you have in the past to get different results.

- Regardless of what happens, say, "PRAISE GOD" to connect with the Source of power, love, and help, and to remember the tools.

- When you get stuck, go back to the toolbelt and find something that will keep you motivated.

- Learn the tools before you get in a crisis situation and need them.

Appendix A
Goal Ladders™

You may copy the forms on the next three pages for your personal use.

Identify a goal.

TM

Prayer Relaxation Attitude Inspiration Self-Talk Energize Others Do Something

TM

 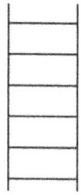 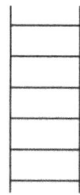

TM

 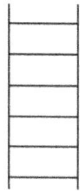 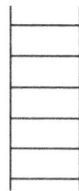

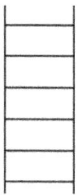 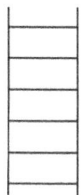 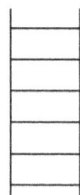

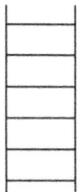 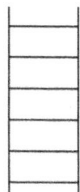 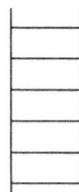

Goal Success Record

Goal: _____

_____

_____

I REACHED MY GOAL!

Date Accomplished: _____

Goal Success Record

Goal: _____

_____

_____

I REACHED MY GOAL!

Date Accomplished: _____

Goal Success Record

Goal: _____

_____

_____

I REACHED MY GOAL!

Date Accomplished: _____

Appendix B
A Child of God

Dr. Edward and Ruth Cowgill
(Dad and Mom)

My folks have both lived lives of service to others. They are my inspiration. Their work has touched thousands of people. Who could have guessed that even their fun, relaxing hobby of writing poetry would continue to touch even more lives?

Earlier I shared three of my Mother's poems. I would like to also share this moving poem my Father wrote. He said he was inspired as he sat in church one Sunday. He went home, wrote it down, and never changed a word.

A CHILD OF GOD

The desert earth was parched and burned,
He stumbled and fell in the dust, we've learned.
'Tis true He fell, seven times they say;
And people jeered along the way.
Across the desert sands they trod
To crucify a child of God.

They were the masses He had come to tell
Of a Spirit within and an escape from Hell.
He knew this would happen, and of course, He cared,
But He wouldn't pray that His life be spared.
And on and up the hill they trod
To crucify a child of God.

And up on the hill they killed all three—
Two thieves and a man from Galilee.
Said the thief on the right, "Take me up with Thee,
Not down from the spikes on the dogwood tree."
This was a child of God they slew
But the thief on the right and the left were, too.

For the power within and the beast without
Were the very things He taught about.
Each time we hate, each time we slay
We join the crowd on that infamous day:
Across the sands on the desert sod
To crucify a child of God.

© 1986 Dr. Edward F. Cowgill

About the Author

Pamela Cowgill holds a B.S. in Applied Communication, Magna Cum Laude, and an Associate Degree in Business Management from Franklin University in Columbus, Ohio.

She has been a writer for 30 years as a documentation specialist, editor, training developer, and technical writer. In recent years, she has had opportunities to do creative writing, produce training videos, and consult with other authors on various types of commercial projects.

This background as well as facing many of life's challenges and suffering from anxiety, stress, and panic attacks led her to create this book and The P.R.A.I.S.E. G.O.D. Toolbelt™.

Notes

[i] Jennifer Thrush, Public Information Officer, Union County Health Department. Published in the Journal-Tribune, Marysville, Ohio. Tuesday, January 18, 2011.

[ii] Ephesians 6:10-20.

[iii] Jack Canfied, Mark Victor Hanson, and LeAnn Thieman. *Chicken Soup for the Soul Answered Prayers, 101 Stories of Hope, Miracles, Faith, Divine Intervention, and the Power of Prayer.* Chicken Soup for the Soul Publishing, LLC., 2011.

[iv] https://www.guideposts.org/

[v] Emoto, Dr. Masaru. *The Healing Power of Water.* Carlsbad, California: Hay House, 2004. Web site: www.hayhouse.com and http://www.masaru-emoto.net/english/e_ome_home.html

[vi] I've heard about adrenalin since I was a child so it is hard to identify the source of this information. There are other chemicals released in your body when you experience stress and anxiety. I'm very familiar with my body's reaction to that. I am not attempting to identify those chemicals. Ask your doctor if you need details.

[vii] Marshall Sylver is the author of *Passion, Profit, and Power.* New York: Simon & Schuster, 1995. Web sites: http://www.simonandschuster.com/ and http://www.sylver.com/

[viii] - Circadian Rhythms Fact Sheet. Web site: http://www.nigms.nih.gov/Publications/Factsheet_CircadianRhythms.htm 07/08/2012

- CDC online publication: http://www.cdc.gov/niosh/pdfs/97-145.pdf 07/08/2012 pp32
- Mercola http://articles.mercola.com/sites/articles/archive/2013/03/19/melatonin-benefits.aspx 01/07/2014

[ix] Information from www.forbes.com published 1/29/2014.

http://www.forbes.com/sites/onmarketing/2014/01/29/yes-a-super-bowl-ad-really-is-worth-4-million/

[x] Beattie, Melodie. *Beyond Codependency.* Center City, Minnesota 55012. Hazelden Foundation, 1989. www.Hazelden.org 1-800-328-9000. Web site: http://melodybeattie.com/

[xi] https://www.skychairs.com/

[xii] Tice, Lou. Web site: http://www.thepacificinstitute.us/v2/index.php

[xiii] Beattie, Melodie. *Beyond Codependency.* (1992) *Codependent No More.* Center City, Minnesota 55012. Hazelden Foundation, 1989. www.Hazelden.org 1-800-328-9000. Web site: http://melodybeattie.com/

xiv Marci Shimoff's website: http://www.happyfornoreason.com/Home.asp

xv Band-Aid™ is a trademarked product, an adhesive bandage with a gauze pad in the center, used to cover minor wounds. https://www.google.com/search?q=band-aid&ie=utf-8&oe=utf-8#q=band-aid+meaning 9/22/2015

xvi Kingston, Karen. *Clear Your Clutter with Feng Shui*. New York, NY: Broadway Books, 1999. Websites: www.spaceclearing.com and http://www.randomhouse.com/crown/broadway-books/

xvii Dr. Robert Schuller. Website: http://www.crystalcathedral.org/

xviii Og Mandino. Website: http://www.ogmandino.com/

xix Cowgill, Ruth. *Edward and Me*. Limited distribution. Out of print.

xx Dr. Seuss. *Oh the Places You Will Go*. New York: Random House, 1990. Web sites: http://www.seussville.com/ and http://www.randomhouse.com/book/43092/oh-the-places-youll-go-by-dr-seuss

xxi Dr. Paul Otte, President of Franklin University, Columbus, Ohio from 1986 to 2008.

xxii Psychology Today. "Make Your Self-Talk Work for You" by Susan Krauss Whitbourne, Ph.D. https://www.psychologytoday.com/blog/fulfillment-any-age/201309/make-your-self-talk-work-you (Posted Sept 10, 2013)

xxiii Peale, Norman Vincent. *The Positive Power of Jesus Christ* (pp. 24). Carmel, NY: Guideposts Edition, 1980.

xxiv Jones, Charles E. *Life is Tremendous*. Wheaton, Illinois: Tyndale House Publishers, 1968. Web site: http://www.tremendouslifebooks.com/Charlie_Tremendous_Jones.asp Comment: "Stinkin' thinkin'" is a phrase coined by Charles "Tremendous" Jones. My family and I heard him speak back in the late 1960s at a Parker Chiropractic Research Foundation seminar in Fort Worth, Texas.

xxv Wikipedia 11/9/2014 http://en.wikipedia.org/wiki/List_of_religious_populations

xxvi Government web site: http://www.choosemyplate.gov/ and http://www.choosemyplate.gov/food-groups/fruits.html 11/9/2014

xxvii Greger M.D., Michael. (Date posted: June 24, 2014) *I Want to be Healthier? Change Your Taste Buds*. http://nutritionfacts.org/2014/06/24/want-to-be-healthier-change-your-taste-buds/ 08/23/2015

xxviii Colbert M.D, Don. *The Bible Cure for Cancer*. Lake Mary, Florida: Siloam, 1999. Colbert M.D, Don. *Eat This and Live*. Lake Mary, Florida: Siloam, 2009.

xxix Mann, Denise. Reviewed by Hansa D. Bhargava, MD. Sleep and Weight Gain. Will better sleep help you avoid extra pounds? http://www.webmd.com/sleep-disorders/excessive-sleepiness-10/lack-of-sleep-weight-gain 08/29/2015

xxx http://www.cdc.gov/sleep/ 07/08/2012

xxxi http://kidshealth.org/teen/your_body/take_care/how_much_sleep.html 11/9/2011

xxxii Reed, Scott. Author of poetry, essays, and satiric novels, b.1938. This quote was found at http://thinkexist.com/quotes/scott_reed/ and http://www.motivatingquotes.com/goalsq.htm accessed 3/11/2012.

xxxiii Ziglar, Zig. Website: http://www.ziglar.com/

xxxiv Sylver, Marshall. Website: http://www.sylver.com/

xxxvxxxv Gretzky, Wayne. Canadian ice hockey player. Web site: http://www.gretzky.com/

xxxvi Thomas Henry Huxley, An Address to the Students of the Faculty of Medicine in
University College, London, May 18, 1870. English biologist. 1825-1895. Quote from http://positivethoughtfortoday.blogspot.com/p/success-quotes.html

xxxvii Gravestoned blog. Web site: http://gravestoned.blogspot.com/

xxxviii Schriver, Sargent. Reference website: http://www.csus.edu/calst/executive/10-11_executive_broch.pdf

xxxix Often attributed to Plato but not verifiable.

xl Stop the Suffering. Web site: www.stopthesuffering.org

xli Maya Angelou's web site: http://mayaangelou.com/

xlii Alice Walker. BrainyQuote.com. Retrieved April 24, 2012, from BrainyQuote.com Web site:
http://www.brainyquote.com/quotes/quotes/a/alicewalke131842.html
Alice Walker is the author of "The Color Purple."
http://alicewalkersgarden.com/

xliii Author unknown. Used by the Girl Scouts of America.
http://www.girlscouts.org/program/gs_central/activity_ideas/songleading.asp

xliv Jeffers, Susan. *Feel the Fear and Do it Anyway*®. New York, NY: Random House, 1988. (Fawcett Books) Web site.:
http://www.susanjeffers.com/home/index.cfm

Scripture taken from the Holy Bible, King James Version®, Reference Edition. Zondervan Bible Publishers of the Zondervan Corporation, Grand Rapids, Michigan, 1977

"Peace I leave with you, my peace I give unto you:
not as the world giveth, give I unto you.
Let not your heart be troubled, neither let it be afraid."
John 14:27